Shadow Work Journal

Copyright © 2021   Robert C. Payton

Contents

Thanks for purchasing this book.
If you enjoy using it, we would
appreciate your review on Amazon.

Shadow Work: What is it?

Many people associate the word "shadow" with gloomy and dismal meanings. As a result, it's tempting to think of shadow work as a grim spiritual exercise involving our personalities' dark and sinister sides.

We are made up of both light and dark parts; the shadow is dark, but it's a part of our identity, and we can't be frightened of it.

The shadow is the unconscious and disowned aspects of our identities that the ego fails to perceive, acknowledge and embrace. It's any part of ourselves that isn't illuminated by the light of our awareness.

We are born entire and complete as children, yet that wholeness is fading. As a result of particular encounters with the individuals closest to us as children, the shadow emerges. Our caregivers convince us that specific characteristics of ourselves are positive and others are negative. The features that are perceived as unfavorable are rejected, resulting in the shadow.

How can your shadow affect you?

We repress the features that are disliked and emphasize the aspects that are acceptable when we rely on our caretakers for survival.

Imagine a sensitive eight-year-old boy. He is soft-hearted, and something makes him cry. "Stop sobbing like a little girl, be a man!" his father responds.
You must have heard or seen this kind of instance multiple times. Because his father feels that sobbing is wrong, he suppresses his son's feelings. As a result, the boy pushes his soft and sensitive side into the background and starts "playing tough." He has problems experiencing things as an adult and refuses to display his feelings, even when it is essential. He suffers in his relationships as a result of this, never allowing himself to be seen entirely.

Another example is a little girl who becomes enraged over something and begins to throw a tantrum. Her mother immediately orders her to "Stop it! Stop being such a jerk!" Every time she gets furious, her mother tells her to calm down and be a nice girl. The small girl grows up with the notion that getting angry is bad, and tries so hard not to become furious. She dissociates from her emotions over time, but this does not make them go away.

She grows up raised with the belief that she must constantly be in control. She later recognizes that she is having problems at work because others are pushing her buttons. She frequently feels as though she is going to burst and has no idea what to do. She recognizes that her anger is always present, manifesting itself in passive-aggressive ways and causing problems at work.

How to do shadow work?

So, how do you go about identifying your shadow? It all comes down to bringing the unconscious mind into our waking consciousness. Psychoanalytic thinkers saw this as crucial to preserving psychological well-being.

It's usually done using the "Socratic method" of inquiry and investigation. Asking objective questions that prompt critical thinking and re-examining past assumptions about ourselves is part of this process.

The concept is that a more objective entity (like a therapist) might assist in holding up an interpretative mirror to the aspects of ourselves that we find difficult to see and accept.

While this is usually done with the guidance of a therapist, you may start exploring your shadow on your own by evaluating your ideas, feelings, and assumptions. You'll find some prompts to assist you below. The elements of ourselves that have been pushed down to the unconscious — the portions that we're anxious about, embarrassed about, or frustrated with, and hence repress — are known as the "shadow self." The shadow self is founded on the idea that we bury those aspects of our personalities that we fear will not be received, accepted, or appreciated by others. Therefore, we keep them hidden in the "shadows." To put it another way, our shadow selves are the versions of ourselves that we don't exhibit to the rest of the world.

What exactly is shadow work? This is the discipline of accepting what is and releasing guilt and judgments so that we can be our authentic selves. The greatest happiness in life is the conviction that we are loved — loved for ourselves, or rather, loved in spite of ourselves.

Benefits you can reap from shadow exercises

The unfortunate fact is that the term "shadow work" brings up all kinds of evil and dark ideas for a lot of individuals. It's natural to think of shadow work as a gloomy spiritual activity because of our connections with the word.

Alternatively, it might be internal work involving solely the more profound negative or dark sides of ourselves. Or perhaps it merely traps you in a state of helplessness and anguish. Or you're worried that if you concentrate just on the darkness, all you'll get is more shadow. All of this, however, is not the case. So let's look at the potential advantages of shadow work.

1. Shadowing is a valuable tool. It's a tool in the same way that focusing on the good is. You can master that tool, just as you can any other device. Working in the shadows isn't a way of life. It isn't something that you experience. It isn't something that takes up all of your time. It's not the whole picture. It's a technique for becoming aware, stepping out of and altering destructive patterns, entering a more objective reality, moving into free will and conscious choice, and thus actively and consciously constructing your existence.

2. Shadow work makes you more aware of your surroundings and allows you to see things. It's learning what you don't know about. It is, in fact, necessary for being conscious, aware, and awakened. It places you directly in the middle of the truth — in fact, in realism. As a result, shadow work may provide practically any advantage that comes from perceiving the truth, having a more objective perspective, being aware, or being in reality.

3. It gives you a sense of power. Your power axis exists in reality, and you can't live in that reality until you're conscious of it. Shadow, on the other hand, denotes a lack of consciousness. It alludes to what you're not aware of, as well as what you've suppressed, rejected, denied, repudiated, and pushed out of your consciousness.

You have a choice when you are aware. This implies you'll be in a position of free will rather than determinism. For example, you may not realize that you continually end up getting in relationships with red flags until you undertake shadow work.

Your early life experiences taught you that love is when someone is suffering and miserable in a relationship but remains because they care so much about the other person. You are then in a position to select compatible persons with whom to form a relationship.

Some people are afraid that doing shadow work would make them suffer even more. However, this will only happen if you begin to see things as they are but are persuaded you either can't or won't alter them.

4. In the gloom, there's a lot of gold. Many individuals believe that the shadow is entirely negative and terrible. Actually, there is a lot that a person doesn't know that is wonderful and enjoyable. Also, there is a lot of pleasant and joyful information that we repress, deny, reject, disavow, and push away from consciousness.

Consider the possibility that you were artistic as a youngster. Consider the case that you were born with the desire to be an artist. However, you were born into a household that was preoccupied with academics and shunned artistic expression.

You may have suppressed, rejected, and denied your creative gift, as well as your purpose, in order to be closer to your family. Shadow work will undoubtedly lead to the rediscovery of your artistic skill as well as your life's purpose.

5. Shadow work results in self-introspection. You become more genuine as a result of it. It makes you realize who you are and what your particular reality is. The process of socialization and trauma that we all eventually go through causes us to fragment, among other things. Our personas are, at their core, phony.

Our personalities are essentially the parts of ourselves that we associate with in order to be secure and away from vulnerability in the particular surroundings and circumstances in which we were reared until we become awake and aware of ourselves. We repress, reject, deny, and abandon the qualities that make us vulnerable or cause us to be judged by others. They become subconscious as a result of this. They are buried outside of our awareness, and we are unaware that they exist, despite being visible to others. This implies that we are not who we believe we are.

Shadow work reveals who you indeed are and what you truly desire. It helps you become more self-aware. Without self-awareness, there is no way to live a happy life. To pick what is best for you, you must first understand and own yourself. The only way to achieve a life of pleasure, happiness, and fulfillment is to choose what is uniquely correct for you.

6. Shadow work is a great way to get out of a rut. You're only genuinely stuck if you have no idea what's going on. To begin solving problems and taking action, you must first understand what is going on. That is accomplished through shadow work.

Many individuals believe that working in the shadows renders them weak. It doesn't... it just forces them to acknowledge their limitations. You are witnessing your limitations and thus, by facing them, you are not them. You are no longer a part of them. If you choose to bring consciousness to impotence, it is no longer powerless by definition because you have added the frequency of free will to it. It makes you aware of patterns and cycles, causing you to disidentify with them and modify them so they don't reoccur and can be changed.

Individually and intergenerationally, people repeat patterns. As a result, the majority of individuals live in a deterministic manner. Over and over, they keep ending up with unavailable relationships. Addiction and abuse patterns and destructive fundamental beliefs are passed down from generation to generation. Over and over again, humanity repeats the same way. Shadow work breaks the cycle, breaks the chain, and allows you to modify these patterns so that you may select your beliefs, behaviors, and life experiences deliberately.

7. Integration is facilitated through shadow work. Peace is achieved via integration. It promotes internal integration, which leads to inner peace, and exterior integration, which leads to personal and global peace. It reverses the fragmentation process, which is the source of so much pain in both your life and the planet. It helps you get closer to your goals so you can achieve them.

8. To begin with, most people believe they know exactly what they want. They don't, though. For example, suppose you were reared in a conservative household that values marriage. In that case, you may believe that marriage is what you really desire, but the only reason you think you want it is for your family's approval.

For instance, we could aspire to be a lawyer, but in reality, we just care about money and social position, and we have a limited understanding of how to obtain these.

Shadow work reveals what you desire and why you want it. It also broadens the scope of what is feasible. Shadow work also shows what is getting in the way of your goals. It displays a level of resistance. Getting what you desire requires resolving such issues.

Consider this scenario: you have no idea why you can't lose weight no matter how hard you try. It's possible that shadow work will disclose that the portion of your consciousness in charge of your body has no desire to lose weight. It wants to be fat because it utilizes fat as a barrier against the world's dangers and as a replacement border. After all, you can't maintain your own goal.

It will be crucial to work with this section of your consciousness to develop a resolution if you want to lose weight. Every diet and fitness regimen will fail unless you do so.

9. Shadow work helps you recognize and overcome your trauma, which is the underlying issue causing the present patterns in your life that are causing you pain and suffering. This is, without a doubt, the most important thing on my list.

Trauma is a condition of the emotional and mental anguish brought on by unresolved suffering. You don't have to be mistreated or go through something that most people would consider a tragedy (such as war, sexual assault, or the death of a loved one) to be traumatized.

Birth in today's mainstream medical institutions is a stressful process. Weaning a baby is a challenging experience. Losing track of one's mother at a supermarket is unpleasant for a three-year-old.

Even the most exemplary parents on the planet will not be able to raise a child without causing them any harm. If we don't have a mechanism to address and thereby integrate the trauma we encounter as children, we will shape our lives and make decisions based on trauma.

10. We also have a propensity to forget about trauma or normalize it. Worse, since this is a mirror-based universe governed by what many refer to as 'the law of attraction,' this universe will continue to provide us additional opportunities to heal our traumas by placing us in similar situations over and over.

They also have a tendency to magnify or become wacky. For example, suppose we never dealt with the fact that our father abandoned us when we were four years old. In that case, we may decide that in order to avoid the agony of loss, we will become ultra-independent and never be linked to anybody again.

We will not only have intimacy troubles as adults as a result of this event, but we will also be forsaken by others. This trend will then worsen because if we are abandoned, we will use this fact to justify our initial decision to push others away before they have a chance to push us away, increasing the likelihood of their abandoning us.

Thus, it spirals into an ever-worsening vicious circle. We have the power to develop a solid, reliable relationship with others in our lives if we can become aware of and address the initial trauma, as well as the changes we made to ourselves as a result. Shadow work may also indicate that problems we believe were settled aren't, and that's why similar events keep recurring in our life.

11. Shadow work forces you to delve far below the surface of things. It connects you to the blueprint, or fundamental level of being, that lies underneath the surface of reality. Your knowledge, depth, capabilities, breadth, and expanse will all improve as a result of this.

It's similar to a two-dimensional human becoming three-dimensional. This allows you to see things that others can't and perform things that others aren't aware are possible. You get more robust as a result. This is why awakened individuals appear to be so much... more.

12. It allows you to be more aware of what you generate and manifest. Many teachers of the law of attraction and manifestation oversimplify this to the point of illiteracy. The power of concentration, purpose, and thinking is immense. The acts that one does to produce are also necessary.

However, in the time and effort it takes you to focus on one thing, your subconscious mind may focus on other things without you even realizing it. This is why an Olympic swimmer can swim and prepare dinner at the same time. Swimming is an entirely subconscious activity. Your conscious mind does not control the majority of your total personal vibration. And your point of attraction is your complete unique vibration.

In a cosmos governed by the law of attraction, this is huge. For example, if you sit down to say the affirmation "I am good enough," that idea will be contending with numerous other, far more ingrained and powerful frequencies, such as "I'm too overweight" and "No one truly wants me." People who believe they are good enough are always the worst types of people.

Your point of attraction is more complicated than whatever you consciously focus on and do. As a result, you have very little influence over what occurs in your life unless you conduct shadow work. Everything seems to happen TO you, and you have no idea why.

You may deliberately adjust and increase your point of attraction by being aware of the contents of your subconscious mind as well as what you don't know about the world and the cosmos.

And the more awake you are, the more mindful you are when it comes to what you think, say, choose, and do. It will seem like you have control over your life and understand why things happen the way they do.

This frees you from the feeling of being a victim. In the same line as creation, creativity is hampered by blocked energy and inauthenticity. Shadow work dissolves those barriers and resistances, allowing your creative potential to flow freely as the energy of conscious awareness passes through you. You become a much more creative person as a result of this.

13. Shadow work aids in the development of effective, healthy, pleasurable, and mindful relationships. Relationships are vital to one's survival. You have other persons with whom you share a connection. Every aspect of your life, including your profession, diet, hobbies, and body, has a relationship with you. As a result, the quality of your connections determines the quality of your life.

Doing shadow work will make it harder for someone to trigger you. As a result, your interpersonal dynamics will become more mature, healthier, and more functional due to your maturation. You could, for example, have a mysterious connection with your child. Shadow work might indicate that you despise tendencies in your kid that you have hidden, denied, or rejected in yourself, such as selfishness

Perhaps you've dismissed your own egoism, and you're giving your life to your husband and children. However, you despise the fact that you're doing so. As a result, you experience animosity towards your child whenever they act in their best interests. This realization may force you to reconsider your decision and begin doing things for yourself.

14. It improves your physical, mental, and emotional health and well-being. Being unaware is difficult and stressful. Denying, repressing, rejecting, disowning, and pushing things away, or attempting to keep a closet door shut while its contents are overflowing, is exhausting and unpleasant.

Simply put, suppression produces weariness and sickness. The health of all of those layers of you will substantially improve as you unleash the repressed energy and enable more of the significance of consciousness to flow through all of them. You'll have extra stamina. Shadow work also gives you a sense of security and power, making you feel on par with life and very much alive.

These are only a few of the advantages of shadowing. The more aware you are of your shadow, the more embodied you are as a conscious person. Without facing and exposing their darkness to the light of consciousness, no one has ever achieved enlightenment. It is now up to individuals to master this tool, which will lead to their liberty.

Get to the Root of your shadow

The ancient Greeks recognized the importance of honoring all aspects of the mind. As a result, these components were revered as gods and goddesses in their own right.

The Greeks recognized that ignoring a god or goddess would result in that god or goddess turning against you and destroying you. Any aspect of ourselves that we reject turns against us. The personal shadow represents a collection of these disowned aspects.

So here's the issue: Without our complete awareness, the shadow can act on its own. It's as if our conscious self switches to autopilot mode, leaving the unconscious in charge. We do things we wouldn't choose to do and then regret it afterward (if we catch it). We say things that we wouldn't usually say. Our facial expressions reveal feelings we aren't aware of.

Our relationships with our spouses, families, and friends will suffer if we remain unaware of the shadow, as will our professional connections and leadership abilities.

How to Recognize Your Own Shadow

Nothing exists in the inherent condition of separation and division. On the contrary, humans are wired for integration and wholeness. Therefore, the subconscious will constantly strive to capture your attention to integrate what's there.

It might be tough to recognize your own shadow, especially if you've pushed a tiny portion of yourself into the unconscious mind. Here are three techniques for detecting your shadow in action:

1. Make a projection

Many individuals blame their problems on others. They point out flaws in others when they detest something about themselves. We frequently project our shadows — repressed anger, remorse, shame, and other aspects of ourselves that we dislike — onto others. Then, we strike out at others because we don't like our own behavior.

Keep an eye on how you present yourself to the rest of the world. People, places, and things become mirrors that reflect who we indeed are while the universe attempts to make us whole again.

2. Reactions

A trigger is a recollection of a previous traumatic event. The surface occurrences that generate tension in our lives are messengers that allow us to become aware of something hidden deep inside us. Please pay attention to your triggers; they might readily reveal your wounds and your shadow. Try to recognize your emotional triggers before acting out rather than afterward.

3. Patterns

Patterns in our life that repeat themselves represent components of our shadow. Because the shadow reflects itself into your reality to be viewed and assimilated, patterns are representations of the shadow.

The shadow wishes for you to notice it. It aspires to be noticed and accepted. You'll uncover components of your shadow self inside these patterns that will continue to crop up in new settings until you're ready to look at them and stop the cycle.

Wound Mapping

Many of our troubles stem from our unwillingness to confront our troubling ideas and feelings. Our inner lives become divided when we avoid acknowledging areas that produce vulnerability. Instead of interpreting our discomfort as either good or bad, we may use the whole range of our human experiences in surprising ways if we turn to confront those thoughts and feelings.

What sets us off, what presses our buttons, might reveal stuff buried in our shadow that must be addressed.

HERE'S A FUN ACTIVITY TO TRY:

Everyday situations that irritate you or push your buttons might cause unintended consequences (feelings and behaviors) that are out of proportion to the event. These are one-of-a-kind to you. However, there is a belief going on in the middle (between the activating situation and your response).

This is the belief that we want to bring to light through coaching. So, give it a go...

Acknowledge your own activating events.
Recognize the activating events that have occurred in your life. Consider the things that happen in your life that truly get you moving. Is it getting stuck in traffic? Is it that your kids aren't doing their chores? Is there a project that has gone over budget? Make a mental note of how much these occurrences affect you.

Activating event 1:

Activating event 2:

Activating event 3:

Now think of the consequences of these actions:

What effect did they have on you?

What exactly did you do?

Now we'll take a step back and consider the following belief: What was going through your mind?

Alternative interpretations are being challenged and created.
Is there a method to put your belief to the test? Is this, for example, a 100 percent accurate interpretation? What proof is there, and where is it? Make a list of any examples or evidence that contradicts your ideas. What evidence does the list support when you think about it?

You imagine other perspectives.
If you discover that your list is biased, you can go further and come up with other ways to interpret the incident. For example, what are the details you're missing? Is there anything else that might be impacting the situation?

Our shadow parts can be integrated by recognizing our triggers and allowing them to lead us to hidden beliefs. We may begin to overcome their hold on our lives and lessen their negative influence and disturbance once we understand them and how they operate.

Positive Quotes

ALL THE BEAUTY OF LIFE IS MADE UP OF LIGHT AND SHADOW.

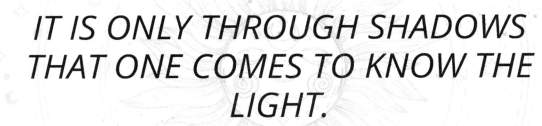

IT IS ONLY THROUGH SHADOWS THAT ONE COMES TO KNOW THE LIGHT.

NEVER FEAR SHADOWS. THEY MEAN THERE'S A LIGHT SHINING SOMEWHERE NEARBY.

Shadow Work Prompts

Date: 2 / 6 / 24 .

Which emotion makes you feel the most uneasy or uncomfortable to sit with? Which one do you try to avoid the most?

ANXIETY.

Today I am grateful for:

MY HOME & FAMILY.

Did I get triggered today? Describe what happended:

previously

Kids + Mike issue .

Date: _____

Think back to a scenario or situation where that emotion played out. What happened? How did you react initially? What other emotions played out alongside the one you tried to avoid?

Had to deal with anxiety on my own. as a child. or deal with Parent(s) anxiety.

Today I am grateful for:

Did I get triggered today? Describe what happended:

Date: _____

What negative emotions are you most comfortable with? Do you cling to certain emotions on a day-to-day basis because they feel 'normal'?

_____

_____

_____

_____

_____

_____

_____

_____

_____

_____

_____

Today I am grateful for:

_____

_____

Did I get triggered today? Describe what happended:

_____

_____

_____

_____

Date: _____

Is your inner voice kind or critical? What things
does it say to you on a typical day?

_____

_____

_____

_____

_____

_____

_____

_____

_____

_____

_____

_____

Today I am grateful for:

_____

_____

Did I get triggered today? Describe what happended:

_____

_____

_____

_____

Date: _____

Is your inner voice truly yours? Whose voice could be influencing your inner voice (parents, partners, teachers, friends, etc.)? Would you say the things that the voice tells you to other people? If not, then those thoughts aren't your authentic voice. Instead, they're reflections of other people's beliefs you've internalized.

_____

_____

_____

_____

_____

_____

_____

_____

Today I am grateful for:

_____

_____

Did I get triggered today? Describe what happended:

_____

_____

_____

_____

Date: _____

Look at your past. Who has or still does regularly downplay how you feel?

_____

_____

_____

_____

_____

_____

_____

_____

_____

_____

_____

_____

Today I am grateful for:

_____

_____

Did I get triggered today? Describe what happended:

_____

_____

_____

_____

Date: _____

"I am easily influenced or swayed by the opinions and beliefs of others. As a result, I find it hard to assert my voice and figure out what is them versus me." Explore this statement.

_____

_____

_____

_____

_____

_____

_____

_____

_____

_____

_____

_____

Today I am grateful for:

_____

_____

Did I get triggered today? Describe what happended:

_____

_____

_____

_____

Date: _____

"I regularly downplay how I feel or what I'm thinking for the sake of others." Do you agree or disagree with this statement?

_____

_____

_____

_____

_____

_____

_____

_____

_____

_____

_____

Today I am grateful for:

_____

_____

Did I get triggered today? Describe what happended:

_____

_____

_____

_____

Date: _____

Why do you let people who don't acknowledge your feelings stay in your life? Do you have a desire to keep their company? Or do you know that there's something you could be doing to make the relationship better?

_____

_____

_____

_____

_____

_____

_____

_____

_____

_____

Today I am grateful for:

_____

_____

Did I get triggered today? Describe what happended:

_____

_____

_____

Date: _____

Do you value yourself and what you bring to the table?

_____

_____

_____

_____

_____

_____

_____

_____

_____

_____

_____

_____

Today I am grateful for:

_____

_____

Did I get triggered today? Describe what happended:

_____

_____

_____

Date: _____

How can you be kinder to yourself? In what
ways do you punish or sabotage yourself?

_____

_____

_____

_____

_____

_____

_____

_____

_____

_____

_____

_____

_____

Today I am grateful for:

_____

_____

Did I get triggered today? Describe what happended:

_____

_____

_____

_____

Date: _____

How important are you to yourself?

_____
_____
_____
_____
_____
_____
_____
_____
_____
_____
_____

Today I am grateful for:

_____

Did I get triggered today? Describe what happended:

_____
_____
_____
_____

Date: _____

Have you ever done something just to make
someone else feel proud of you? If so, who was it,
and why?

_____

_____

_____

_____

_____

_____

_____

_____

_____

_____

_____

Today I am grateful for:

_____

_____

Did I get triggered today? Describe what happended:

_____

_____

_____

_____

Date: _____

Do you fully celebrate your achievements? Or is there a disconnect between your accomplishments and who you are as a person? Which one resonates more?

_____

_____

_____

_____

_____

_____

_____

_____

_____

_____

_____

Today I am grateful for:

_____

_____

Did I get triggered today? Describe what happended:

_____

_____

_____

_____

Date: _____

What is your biggest regret to date?

_____

_____

_____

_____

_____

_____

_____

_____

_____

_____

_____

_____

Today I am grateful for:

_____

_____

Did I get triggered today? Describe what happended:

_____

_____

_____

_____

Date: _____

Imagine you're coming to the end of your life. What is the biggest regret you fear having the most? How does that make you feel, and where does it sit within the body?

_____

_____

_____

_____

_____

_____

_____

_____

_____

_____

_____

Today I am grateful for:

_____

_____

Did I get triggered today? Describe what happended:

_____

_____

_____

_____

Date: _____

Imagine your worst fear came true. How does
that make you feel now about your life ahead?

_____

_____

_____

_____

_____

_____

_____

_____

_____

_____

_____

Today I am grateful for:

_____

_____

Did I get triggered today? Describe what happended:

_____

_____

_____

_____

Date: _____

Imagine your most wanted dream came true right now. How does that make you feel about your life ahead? Are there similar feelings and emotions tied to both your fears and successes?

_____

_____

_____

_____

_____

_____

_____

_____

_____

_____

_____

Today I am grateful for:

_____

Did I get triggered today? Describe what happended:

_____

_____

_____

Date: _____

Do you feel you're only as good as your last achievement? If yes, why? If no, why not?

_____

_____

_____

_____

_____

_____

_____

_____

_____

_____

_____

_____

Today I am grateful for:

_____

_____

Did I get triggered today? Describe what happended:

_____

_____

_____

_____

Date: _____

What do you think are your most undesirable traits and characteristics? (This is NOT an opportunity to put yourself down, but rather a chance to unearth what you believe to be true about yourself. This doesn't mean what you write is an accurate reflection of yourself.)

_____
_____
_____
_____
_____
_____
_____
_____
_____
_____

Today I am grateful for:

_____
_____

Did I get triggered today? Describe what happended:

_____
_____
_____
_____

Date: _____

What image do you think other people have of you?

_____

_____

_____

_____

_____

_____

_____

_____

_____

_____

_____

_____

Today I am grateful for:

_____

_____

Did I get triggered today? Describe what happended:

_____

_____

_____

_____

Date: _____

How would you like others to describe you? Is there a difference between your answer to this question and the previous one? How does that make you feel?

_____
_____
_____
_____
_____
_____
_____
_____
_____
_____
_____
_____

Today I am grateful for:

_____
_____

Did I get triggered today? Describe what happended:

_____
_____
_____
_____

Date: _____

"If I could be anything in the world, I would be..."
Fill in the blank.

_____

_____

_____

_____

_____

_____

_____

_____

_____

_____

_____

_____

Today I am grateful for:

_____

_____

Did I get triggered today? Describe what happended:

_____

_____

_____

_____

Why aren't you already doing the thing you mentioned in the above question? What's stopping you?

_____

_____

_____

_____

_____

_____

_____

_____

_____

_____

_____

_____

Today I am grateful for:

_____

_____

Did I get triggered today? Describe what happended:

_____

_____

_____

_____

Date: _____

What is your definition of failure?

_____
_____
_____
_____
_____
_____
_____
_____
_____
_____
_____
_____

Today I am grateful for:

_____

Did I get triggered today? Describe what happended:

_____
_____
_____
_____

Date: _____

"When I think back to a time that I failed, I feel…" Fill in the blank.

_____

_____

_____

_____

_____

_____

_____

_____

_____

_____

_____

_____

_____

Today I am grateful for:

_____

_____

Did I get triggered today? Describe what happended:

_____

_____

_____

_____

Date: _____

What is your definition of perfection? Is it attainable?

_____
_____
_____
_____
_____
_____
_____
_____
_____
_____
_____
_____
_____
_____

Today I am grateful for:

_____
_____

Did I get triggered today? Describe what happended:

_____
_____
_____
_____

Date: _____

Do you hold yourself to a higher standard than you do others? If so, why?

_____

_____

_____

_____

_____

_____

_____

_____

_____

_____

_____

_____

Today I am grateful for:

_____

_____

Did I get triggered today? Describe what happended:

_____

_____

_____

_____

Date: _____

In what areas of your life do you feel inferior to others?

_____

_____

_____

_____

_____

_____

_____

_____

_____

_____

_____

_____

Today I am grateful for:

_____

_____

Did I get triggered today? Describe what happended:

_____

_____

_____

_____

Date: _____

Have you ever sacrificed a part of yourself to fit in with others better?

_____
_____
_____
_____
_____
_____
_____
_____
_____
_____
_____

Today I am grateful for:

_____
_____

Did I get triggered today? Describe what happended:

_____
_____
_____
_____

Date: _____

Where are you playing small in your life?

_____
_____
_____
_____
_____
_____
_____
_____
_____
_____
_____
_____

Today I am grateful for:

_____
_____

Did I get triggered today? Describe what happended:

_____
_____
_____
_____

Date: _____

What narrative or stories do you tell yourself
surrounding 'wanting more'?

_____
_____
_____
_____
_____
_____
_____
_____
_____
_____
_____
_____
_____

Today I am grateful for:

_____
_____

Did I get triggered today? Describe what happended:

_____
_____
_____
_____

Date: _____

"If I could tell my younger self only one thing, it would be…" Fill in the blank.

_____

_____

_____

_____

_____

_____

_____

_____

_____

_____

_____

_____

Today I am grateful for:

_____

_____

Did I get triggered today? Describe what happended:

_____

_____

_____

_____

Date: _____

When have you felt abandoned by those
around you? Describe the situation and what
it made you think.

_____

_____

_____

_____

_____

_____

_____

_____

_____

_____

_____

Today I am grateful for:

_____

_____

Did I get triggered today? Describe what happended:

_____

_____

_____

_____

Date: _____

How do you show up for others in ways that you don't show up for yourself?

_____
_____
_____
_____
_____
_____
_____
_____
_____
_____
_____
_____

Today I am grateful for:

_____
_____

Did I get triggered today? Describe what happended:

_____
_____
_____
_____

Date: _____

What do you need to forgive yourself for?

_____
_____
_____
_____
_____
_____
_____
_____
_____
_____
_____
_____

Today I am grateful for:

_____
_____

Did I get triggered today? Describe what happended:

_____
_____
_____
_____

Date: _____

"I feel the need to keep myself hidden and small for the sake of others' feelings." Explore this statement.

_____
_____
_____
_____
_____
_____
_____
_____
_____
_____
_____
_____
_____

Today I am grateful for:

_____
_____

Did I get triggered today? Describe what happended:

_____
_____
_____
_____

Date: _____

"I've stayed in relationships (either platonic or romantic) that deep down I knew weren't good for me. Why did I do that?" Explore this statement and the feelings it brings up.

_____

_____

_____

_____

_____

_____

_____

_____

_____

_____

Today I am grateful for:

_____

_____

Did I get triggered today? Describe what happended:

_____

_____

_____

_____

Date: _____

"I am worthy of good things coming my way." Do you agree or disagree, and why?

_____

_____

_____

_____

_____

_____

_____

_____

_____

_____

_____

_____

Today I am grateful for:

_____

_____

Did I get triggered today? Describe what happended:

_____

_____

_____

_____

Date: _____

How would you feel and why if you were to live the remaining years of your life as an exact repeat of what has gone by? Where would you make changes?

_____

_____

_____

_____

_____

_____

_____

_____

_____

_____

_____

Today I am grateful for:

_____

_____

Did I get triggered today? Describe what happended:

_____

_____

_____

_____

Date: _____

Describe the time when you felt the most alone.

_____
_____
_____
_____
_____
_____
_____
_____
_____
_____
_____
_____
_____

Today I am grateful for:

_____
_____

Did I get triggered today? Describe what happended:

_____
_____
_____
_____

Date: _____

"In the past, I have let people take advantage of me." Explore this statement.

_____
_____
_____
_____
_____
_____
_____
_____
_____
_____
_____
_____

Today I am grateful for:

_____

Did I get triggered today? Describe what happended:

_____
_____
_____
_____

Date: _____

Does acknowledging that other people have taken advantage of you bring up any anger, resentment, or discomfort? If you could turn back the clock, what would you do differently?

_____
_____
_____
_____
_____
_____
_____
_____
_____
_____
_____

Today I am grateful for:

_____
_____

Did I get triggered today? Describe what happended:

_____
_____
_____
_____

Date: _____

Where do you need to set better boundaries in your life?

_____
_____
_____
_____
_____
_____
_____
_____
_____
_____
_____
_____
_____

Today I am grateful for:

_____
_____

Did I get triggered today? Describe what happended:

_____
_____
_____
_____

Date: _____

Did your parents always address and meet
your needs as a child?

_____
_____
_____
_____
_____
_____
_____
_____
_____
_____
_____
_____
_____
_____

Today I am grateful for:

_____
_____

Did I get triggered today? Describe what happended:

_____
_____
_____
_____

Date: _____

Did your teachers and school peers treat you with
the respect and love you deserved as a child?

_____

_____

_____

_____

_____

_____

_____

_____

_____

_____

_____

Today I am grateful for:

_____

_____

Did I get triggered today? Describe what happended:

_____

_____

_____

_____

Date: _____

Thinking back to a time in your childhood when you felt different or outcast, do you notice any similarities between that moment and how you go about your daily life now? Are there childhood fears appearing in your adult life?

_____
_____
_____
_____
_____
_____
_____
_____
_____
_____
_____

Today I am grateful for:

_____
_____

Did I get triggered today? Describe what happended:

_____
_____
_____
_____

Date: _____

What makes you so angry that you don't tell
anyone and instead internalize and bury it?

_____

_____

_____

_____

_____

_____

_____

_____

_____

_____

_____

Today I am grateful for:

_____

_____

Did I get triggered today? Describe what happended:

_____

_____

_____

_____

Date: _____

What do you think about yourself when people say they love you?

_____

_____

_____

_____

_____

_____

_____

_____

_____

_____

_____

Today I am grateful for:

_____

_____

Did I get triggered today? Describe what happended:

_____

_____

_____

_____

Date: _____

Do you fear that other people may see your hidden anxiety or insecurity?

_____

_____

_____

_____

_____

_____

_____

_____

_____

_____

_____

_____

Today I am grateful for:

_____

Did I get triggered today? Describe what happended:

_____

_____

_____

_____

Notes

Notes

Notes

Notes

Notes

Notes

Notes

Notes

Notes

Notes

Printed in Great Britain
by Amazon

42556102R00050

OPERATION ANTARCTICA

WILLIAM MEIKLE

SEVERED PRESS
HOBART TASMANIA

OPERATION ANTARCTICA

Copyright © 2017 William Meikle

WWW.SEVEREDPRESS.COM

ISBN: 978-1-925711-52-3

- 1 -

Captain John Banks' mind reeled with the information he'd just been given. Huddled against the cold, he stood on the deck of the icebreaker wondering what to tell the squad. The Southern Cross hung high in the sky amid a blanket of stars, and away on the horizon the white wall of the ice shelf that was their destination was clearly visible in the twilight that passed for full nighttime at this time of year. The vessel's sharp prow cleaved the waves, and they made good time through clear water, with the long ribbon of their wash trailing behind to the horizon, a glistening silver smear on the water.

Lossiemouth, London, the Azores, the Falklands and now here, right on the verge of Antarctica. It had proved to be a long, tiring trip already. Thirty-six hours ago, the colonel had said jump, and S-Squad jumped; Banks, Sergeant Hynd, Corporal McCally, and five old hands from those available for immediate assignment. Banks knew Wiggins and Parker from Afghanistan, good men both. The other three were new to him, but if they were on the rotation, they had the training and they knew the drill. He had no worries on that score. The only thing he was worried about was being laughed out of the room when he told them what had been thought important enough to subject them to the trip.

He couldn't put it off any longer – the chill breeze on deck was persistent and threatened to freeze his breath at his nose and lips. He had a long look at the approaching ice shelf, a wall that stretched in a ribbon across the horizon, and wondered what was waiting for them there.

*

He got exactly the reaction he'd been expecting.

"Fucking Nazi UFO bases? In Antarctica? Dinnae talk shite. You're having us on, Cap. Aren't you? This is some Indiana Jones Hollywood bollocks, surely? If not that, it's certainly tin-foil hat territory."

Since the mission off Baffin Island, McCally had taken on the role of squad skeptic, one that fitted his stoic Highland nature only too well. He sat at the far end of the table in the cramped cabin that was doubling as their briefing room, a wide grin on his face. Banks smiled in return and sipped at a steaming mug of black coffee before replying, grateful for the warmth both at his chilled hands, and in his gullet and belly.

"I'm only telling you what I was just told on the comms link. The colonel didn't look like he was taking the piss, and although the uplink was a bit dodgy and pixilated most of the time, I could hear him loud and clear."

"I blame the fucking aliens," Wiggins said, and got a laugh all around before Banks called for quiet.

"Listen up, I don't have time to repeat it. Our destination is on Queen Maude Land. The Norwegians have given us dispensation to go in and have a look; it's their territory nowadays, but the Jerries were here first, and were building on and under the ice from 1938 onward. The story is they established a research base, a quiet spot where they could test new forms of propulsion. The rumor, and it's one the colonel sees to give credence to, is that they got a working saucer going before they went quiet."

"Went quiet? What does that mean?" Hynd asked.

"Nobody knows. One summer they were there, the next summer they weren't. And during the war, everybody was too busy to go and look. The Yanks were interested enough to send a team down in the late 40s, but they retreated when their radiation meters went off the scale before they even got ashore. We've been told to be just as careful."

"Good job I'm wearing my lead-lined boxers, then,"

Wiggins replied. "But why now, Cap? What's changed?"

"Something showed up in infra-red on a satellite pass," Banks replied. "The brass is worried that somebody else, the Russians maybe, have gone in to see if there's anything worth plundering."

"And the last thing we want is fucking commie UFOs," Hynd replied, and laughed bitterly. "So we get to freeze our balls off again, Cap? Can you not get us a wee job in the Bahamas? If they want us to investigate weird shit, I vote for the Bermuda Triangle next time."

"Me too, Sarge. Me too," Banks said.

"So, this radiation, Cap," McCally chipped in. "Should we be worried?"

"They sent a drone over with a counter earlier," Banks replied. "We've been given the all clear, and as I said, we've been told to be careful. We'll be wearing detectors; and Wiggins has got his magic knickers. You'll be fine."

"And no fucking aliens, right?"

Banks sighed.

"As far as anybody knows, they built a saucer but never got it off the ice. If they got further on with the research and got it working, I think Von Braun might have known, told the Yanks about it, and we'd already have saucers everywhere."

"We already do," Wiggins replied, "according to some." He lapsed into an atrocious American accent. "Chariots of the Gods, man. They practically own South America."

That got another laugh around the table. Banks stood up.

"Right, that's enough of that bollocks. Roll call in ten on deck. Time to get kitted up."

Hynd stayed behind when the others left and looked Banks in the eye.

"There's more to this than you've let on, isn't there, Cap?"

Banks nodded.

"But it's more rumor and speculation rather than hard fact," he replied. "Nothing to worry the squad with until we know better."

"But it could go sideways on us fast?"

Banks nodded again.

"Doesn't everything? That's why they pay us the big bucks."

Hynd snorted as the two men headed for the storeroom and their kit.

"Remember, Cap, the Caribbean next time. At least we'll be warm when we get shafted."

*

Banks met the squad on deck at the top of the hour. Hughes, Patel, and Wilkes, the three he hadn't worked with before, were in a huddle at the portside gunwales, smoking cigarettes cupped, sailor style, inside their palms. He's noticed that the three, although efficient enough, and pleasant enough company in the mess, kept to a tight group. He knew why too; combat does that to men and these three had served together in some rough spots. He'd read the reports, and knew that he, Hynd, and McCally shared a similar bond. When you go through hell and come out the other side, you remember who helped you get through it.

He called the team together. They all wore white parkas, had rifles slung, and carried small packs on their backs. They were going in light; no need for heavy gear with the icebreaker at anchor just offshore. Their dinghy was already in the water, a fifteen-foot Zodiac with fiberglass hull and twin five hundred cc Honda engines; more than enough power to get them across the half mile of water and around a promontory to the bay that was their destination.

"We're going in quiet and dark, or as dark as we can anyway," he said. "Just in case there's another team already there ahead of us. The icebreaker's going to sit offshore here out of sight and wait for our return. We've got twelve hours to get in and out."

"No personal radios?" Hynd asked.

"Nope. Silent means silent this time. There's a radio on the dinghy's dashboard, and I've got the boat's frequency," he said, and tapped his brow, "so if we need to make a call, we can. But let's hope we don't need to. A quick shufti, see what's what, and back here in time for breakfast. Okay?"

"Yeah," McCally replied. "Like that ever works out to plan."

"Change the patter, Cally," Hynd said. "It's getting on my tits."

"Which is more than your wife ever does, or so I've heard, Sarge," Wiggins replied, and Banks took it as a good omen that they were all still laughing as they went in single file down the ladder to the dinghy.

*

It was colder still down at sea level, and the squad huddled as tightly as they could around the center of the dinghy to avoid both the biting wind off the waves and the splashing spray that turned to slush on the rubber sides.

Hynd took charge of the piloting, keeping the revs so low that they ran nearly silent across the still waters. There was no banter among the men now. The mission had started as soon as they left the deck and they all had a still, tense expression, coiled and ready for any action required.

Banks pulled on his night-vision goggles. They were not that much more effective than normal sight in the twilight, but they had the added advantage of a zoom function that Banks turned to its fullest extent. As Hynd brought the dinghy cruising around the promontory, he got his first sight of the base ahead.

It didn't look like much, just a metal jetty on the shoreline, then up to a pathway that led between half a dozen small metal huts. Beyond that, the ice rose in a dome that might be artificial, but looked natural. Beyond that was only a rocky range of windswept hills and beyond that again, the main bulk of the ice sheet, some half a mile high. It looked more like a summer camp for fishermen than any kind of research station.

As they approached shore, Banks checked the radiation detector at his chest. Red meant danger, but the upper circle of the badge was still solid green. He gave Hynd the thumbs-up, and the sarge brought the dinghy in and alongside the rickety jetty.

The metal of the structure looked pitted and rusted, almost eaten through in places, but they managed to find a spot that appeared firm enough to tie up on. Hynd sent Wiggins up the short ladder first.

"Up you go, fat boy," he said. "If it'll take your lardy arse, it'll do for the rest of us."

"If I've got a lardy arse, it's your wife's fault, Sarge," Wiggins said as he climbed up. "Every time I screw her, she gives me a biscuit."

Hynd slapped the private on the back of his thighs.

"Button your lip, lad," he said. "And climb. We're on the clock here."

Wiggins climbed up onto the surface of the jetty and gingerly tested his footing before turning back.

"We're okay, as long as we don't jump up and down. Or have to service the sarge's missus."

By the time Banks got up out of the dinghy, Wiggins was already making his way to the shore to avoid getting a clout on the ear.

*

The small encampment didn't look any more enticing from closer up. The metal sheds were in better shape than the jetty, but they too showed sign of corrosion and neglect, and there were no other footprints but those of the squad in the snow. The path ahead of them was smooth, white, and pristine

If there is another team here, they didn't come this way.

At least it wasn't particularly cold. There was no wind to speak of now that they were off the bay and out of the water, and it would be full dawn soon and warm up farther. Banks guessed it couldn't be much more than a degree or two below freezing.

"Cheer up, Cap," Hynd said. "At least it's not Baffin Island."

"Don't fucking remind me," Hynd said, and meant it. They'd lost three good men in that cluster-fuck. He wasn't in any mood to recreate the memory. He motioned for McCally to take Wiggins and Parker to the sheds on the right, while he, Hynd, Hughes, Patel, and Wilkes went left.

The door of the first shed was hanging almost off its hinges. Inside, a space the size of a family-car garage, there were two rows of wooden crates, each stamped with a swastika, all still nailed down as if they'd been stored after transit and never opened. A thick layer of frost lay over everything, and again there were no footprints on the floor or around the doorway, no sign that anyone had been here for decades. A single bare electric bulb hung overhead. Patel pulled a string cord at the side of the door, and it came off in his hand, falling in three parts to the floor. He got a clout around the ear from Hynd.

"Behave yourself, lad," Hynd said. "Save the farting about for when we get back."

Patel had the good sense to look abashed, and all five of them kept quiet as they left the empty building and moved uphill to the second shed. Banks looked over to his right to see McCally give a thumbs-down at the door of the shed he'd been sent to investigate.

Looks like this will be a short trip.

Banks checked his radiation badge again, relieved to see that it still showed green, then led the other four to the door of the second shed. This one was in better condition, the heavy double door solid and locked against them, not giving way under a hard shoulder shove from Wiggins. But it opened easily enough after the sarge got into the lock with a small pick.

This shed was better insulated than the first, with a timber interior wall. It was, or rather had been, living quarters, with two beds to the right, a table and three chairs in the center, and a large stove against the left wall for heating and cooking. One of the beds looked almost lumpy, and Banks' first thought was that it must be a body, but when Hynd checked, it was just a bundle of crumpled sheets and blankets. Everything was neat, tidied away, except for a newspaper on the table. It only had a light cover of frost, easily wiped away, and although it was in German, the date was clear enough – November 29th, 1942.

There was a pair of tall lockers, military-style, beside the beds, but they were empty save for some frozen-solid woolens. Reading the room, Banks guessed that the occupants had simply put on their cold weather clothing and left one day, never to return.

They did a quick survey of every corner, but came up with nothing more than what they had already. When they got outside, McCally was at the door of another shed, and once again gave a thumbs-down.

Banks was more and more convinced they were on a wild goose chase.

*

Any thoughts of a wasted journey were blown away at the third hut. This one was far more solidly built and resembled the other sheds on the hillside, but only in so far as it had been made to look that way from a distance. It had been painted the same institutional green, but it was made of iron rather than thin sheet metal, and rang like the hull of a boat when hit by the butt of a rifle. Similarly, the door wasn't a door as such, but more of a hatch, like an interior entranceway on a boat or a sub.

McCally brought his team up to join the rest of the squad, and Wiggins tried to turn the metal wheel to engage the locking mechanism. It squealed, but didn't give.

"Give us a hand here, somebody," he said. "This bastard's playing hard to get."

Parker was first to move, and once both men took a side of the wheel, it moved more easily. The screech of metal on metal echoed around the still bay, causing Banks to look around, checking that the sound had not brought them to anyone's attention. The door swung outward with another ear-piercing shriek, showing darkness beyond, and a set of metal stairs leading down into the hill, heading inland.

Banks had another look around the bay. Nothing moved; even the water was still and the dinghy sat calmly at its berth. A dome of clear sky hung overhead, the stars fading out and disappearing as the sun began a slow climb over the horizon. Banks had a last gaze at the sun, cursing it for its promise of heat, then turned back to the dark hole beyond the door. He checked his radiation badge and was relieved to see it was still in the green.

"Okay, Cally, you're on point. Take us in."

The corporal stepped forward, then immediately stopped, and waved Banks up alongside him to look down the stairwell. Banks saw that they'd need both night-vision goggles and the lights on their rifle once inside fully, but he didn't need either to see six steps down.

A body lay sprawled on the first landing.

- 2 -

The corridor was only wide enough for two of them to pass abreast at a time. Banks went down first ahead of Parker and Hynd to stand over the body beside McCally. Some thin light filtered down from above, but not enough for a clear view of the body. He pulled down his goggles.

The Swastika armband stood out sharp and clear in the night vision, leaving Banks in no doubt about the man's allegiance even despite the layer of frost that covered the corpse from head to toe. He wasn't a soldier; he wore a set of thick canvas overalls, stout boots, had a pair of heavy-rimmed spectacles frozen to his face, and he wasn't wearing any headgear. The sleeves of his shirt were rolled up as far as his elbows.

"He's not wearing any cold weather gear, Cap," McCally said, stating the obvious. This man had been working in warmer conditions than they currently faced. Then he'd been struck down, but there was no obvious cause of death, nor any wounds of any kind. There hadn't been any voiding of body fluids either. It looked like he'd set himself down to sleep on the landing, then froze – and quickly at that – in place.

Banks looked up to the roof. They were in a man-made tunnel that looked to be of the same iron as the door to the outside. Strips of what must be lighting, and possible heating, ran the length of the ceiling, all currently dark, and with the same thin layer of frost covering everything.

"A sudden loss of power, maybe?" McCally said. "Would that do it?"

Banks looked down at the body again.

"Even down here it wouldn't happen that fast. He'd have had time to try to get somewhere warmer. It looks like he just gave up on the spot. Went to sleep and froze to death."

He waved his light down the stairs ahead. They kept going into the darkness, with no bottom in sight, and a cold waft of stale air came up from below.

"Gloves on, lads, and hoods up. It's going to get a tad chilly from here on in."

*

He was right behind McCally as they went down, thirty steps before they reached the bottom. There hadn't been any more corpses on the stairs, but there were more here. They lay in doorways, on floors, slumped against walls, strewn throughout the large open chamber in which the squad found themselves.

The ceiling was a few feet above their heads, with more of the lighting strips stretching over it, all as frosted as the ones they'd seen in the stairwell on the way down. The chamber appeared to be the central hub of the underground system, with a dozen doors in a circle around it. Some of the doors were closed, others open, but with only darkness showing beyond them, too far away for their lights to penetrate the shadows. Banks counted the bodies, twelve in all, and all of which looked as rested, composed, and dead, as the one up on the landing by the door. To a man, they appeared to have stopped whatever business they'd been about and died, with no sign of stress or injury.

And that's just the ones I can see. What the fuck happened here?

Eleven of the doors off the chamber were single-sized, but there was one double door and after taking his bearings, Banks knew that must lead deeper again into the ice, toward where he'd seen the domed area between the huts and the hills. If they were going to find anything, he had a hunch it would be through there.

But better to be safe than sorry.

"I want a sweep of all these rooms," he said. "Leave the large door for last – I've got a feeling we'll be going through there soon enough. But make sure the rest of the rooms are clear. And if you find any documentation, any books or papers, shout out and I'll come running. And Wiggins..."

The hefty private looked up as Banks shone a light on him.

"Aye, Cap?"

"Don't touch anything you shouldn't. And keep your trousers on, lad. Wouldn't want your bollocks to drop off, would we?"

*

They split into the same teams as they'd used to search the sheds outside. McCally took his team off clockwise, and Banks went the other way. Banks' first stop was at a long row of lockers against the walls; a quick examination found they contained a mixture of cold weather gear and weaponry – vintage pistols and rifles in the main, everything covered in the same white frosting.

They moved on and quickly discovered that of the eleven rooms, eight were sleeping quarters, six bunks to a room. They found more corpses, half of the bunks occupied by the same, strangely calm, frozen dead. Banks noted that they were all men, and equally split between civilians and military judging by the uniforms on some, overalls on others.

Of the remaining three rooms, one was a mess hall, a cramped set of six tables and long benches, and a large kitchen and storage area at the rear beyond a serving trestle. Banks went over to check the tall cupboards. He found a freezer, almost empty save for lumps of ice that might be meat, and a larger packed with decades-old tins of vegetables and fruit, many of which had burst. There were no bodies here, just more of the thin covering of frost and a terrible sense of emptiness.

"What the fuck happened here, Cap?" Wiggins whispered.

"That's what we're trying to find out, lad."

The second to last room Banks led his team to was obviously a generator and electrical area; he recognized what must be a fuse panel, gauges that registered voltage, and a cubic metal box that he took to be the base's generator, but looked like nothing he'd ever seen before. Along the far wall, there was a series of tall metal containers and cabling, looking more like a farmer's milking system than anything remotely electrical. A thicker cable led off, through the wall and away, heading further into the ice.

Banks turned to the team.

"Wiggins, Parker, see if you can make head or tail of this; maybe even get it up and running. We could do with a heat, or barring that, even some light would be nice to save us wandering about here in the gloaming."

He left the two men in the generator room and headed to the last door. The handle felt icy cold even through his gloves, and he had to put his shoulder to the door. It scraped, ice on metal, as it opened.

This wasn't a dorm, but an officer's quarters. There was a proper bed at the far end of the room, but the occupant wasn't in it; he was sitting upright in a chair at a writing desk. Banks knew this must be the base commander, and the man was definitely military; the black uniform, stiff hat, and bright red swastika armband all clearly visible even under the frost layer. His insignia told Banks his rank had been Oberstleutnant, a Wing Commander. The fact that he was a Luftwaffe officer, in Antarctica, was the first sign they'd had that there might be something to find here after all.

*

The officer looked to have been in his fifties, clean-shaven bar a pencil moustache as black as his uniform jacket. His eyes were now little more than frozen, milky marbles set back in their sockets but apart from that, he looked as if he might stand at any moment after having had a nap.

The desk itself was strewn with notebooks, maps, papers, and diagrams. Banks brushed the ice off one, a nicely bound leather journal, and opened it. Although the rest of the papers on the desk all seemed to be written in German, much to his surprise, this particular book was written in English. One name toward the bottom of the first page immediately caught his eye.

From the personal journal of Thomas Carnacki, 472 Cheyne Walk, Chelsea.

As I have mentioned elsewhere in these journals, there are several of my cases I cannot relate to Dodgson and the others at all. Some of them involve maintaining a degree of delicacy and decorum. For example, there is a great lady of the land who would be most embarrassed should details of her involuntary nocturnal wanderings ever become public.

But there are other cases, often dark, often furtive, that I must by rights keep close to my chest. This is not because they are too alarming or disturbing for my good friends, but purely because if I did tell anyone, I would in all probability meet my end in a dark cell on bread and water for the rest of my natural life. That is, if I did not see the end of a hangman's rope first. Matters of national security are tricky things at the best of times, and when they call for my peculiar area of expertise, they tend to become even more peculiar still and even less available for public consumption.

My friend, Dodgson, has written elsewhere of my infrequent encounters with the extraordinary Mr. Winston Churchill, and the matter I will relate here begins, and ends, with one such meeting.

"The plot thickens," Banks whispered to himself. He needed to know more, but before he had time for that, he needed to know what was beyond the big double door.

A leather satchel sat on the floor at the dead oberst's feet, and Banks quickly gathered up all the papers and notebooks and stowed them away, before stowing the satchel itself in his backpack, feeling the weight of history on his shoulders.

While Banks was stowing the papers, Hynd had been

checking the desk drawers.

"Nothing important in here, Cap," he said. "Fresh paper and ink, frozen solid. There doesn't seem to be a log or report book."

"It'll be around somewhere," Banks replied. "And that's something we'll definitely want."

He had a last look at the officer in the chair – he still couldn't believe the man wasn't going to get up and walk. There was only one other thing of note, a calendar hanging on the wall by the door with one date circled heavily in red pencil.

4th of January, 1942.

*

McCally and his team arrived from across the chamber as Banks and Hynd left the officer's room.

"Anything, Cally?"

The corporal shook his head.

"More dead men in their beds. Looks like whatever did it took them nice and quiet in their sleep. It's a fucking mystery all right."

So far, they had not found a single sign that there had been any warning at all given to the residents of the base. It appeared they had all died in the same moment, some going about whatever their business might be and others, possibly a different work shift, being taken in their beds. Banks hoped an answer might be forthcoming on the other side of the big double door.

Before broaching it, he walked over to the generator room doorway and called out to the two men working inside.

"Any joy, Wiggins?" he asked.

The private looked glum.

"Nothing doing, Cap," he said. He pointed his light at the thicker wiring that ran through the wall. "We thought the generator might be here to feed power through yon cable there. But it's the other way round. It's all dead in here, and any juice to run this beastie would be coming from wherever that goes."

On the other side of the double doors.

"Saddle up then, lads," Banks said. "Let's find out what these buggers were all so busy at before they died."

- 3 -

The double doors weren't locked and opened easily enough, although the creaking of the hinges echoed like a wailing siren around the chamber and brought the hackles rising at the back of Bank's neck. His gut was telling him to run away, and over the years, he'd learned to trust it. But he had a job to do here, and a team to lead.

"Cally, you're on point. Parker and Wiggins, watch our backs. We don't know what killed these Jerries, so if you see anything squirrelly, you have my permission to shoot it."

McCally led Hughes, Patel, and Wilkes into the darkness beyond the door, with Banks and Hynd following right behind them.

It became obvious quickly that they were in a long, enclosed tunnel. There were no doors to either side, just an alley of darkness stretching away beyond the range of their lights. It was colder still in here, and the darkness felt heavier, more oppressive. The floor rose upward at a slight incline, and Banks' mental map of the area told him that they must be travelling up toward the domed area of ice they'd seen from the outside.

The corridor was made of the same metal plating they'd seen throughout the facility, and again Banks was reminded more of the interior of a boat than an under the ice base. The heating costs in fuel while the place was operational must have been enormous. That had him wondering, not for the first time, what was so important to the Nazi effort that could lead them to such secrecy and expense.

And in a project that has obviously failed.

He hoped to find an answer at the end of the corridor.

*

The corridor itself continued for fifty more paces. There were no more corpses, but as they approached another double door, they saw thin, watery, light coming through the small eye-level windows in the doors themselves. Banks didn't have to give the order; all of the squad unslung their rifles into their hands and their level of alertness went up a notch. They moved as one toward the doorway.

Banks stepped forward to try to peer through, but the windows were frosted over. He managed to clear his side, but the inside was still too milky and opaque. He could make out a large darker shadow beyond, but nothing to say what might lie on the other side. He motioned for silence and they stood quiet, listening, but all he heard was the team's own breathing. He motioned for McCally to come forward, and covered the corporal as he slowly pushed the door open.

Once again, a creaking wail of old hinges echoed loud all around them. All attempts at secrecy were now moot. Banks gave the signal, and the squad, as one, moved forward through the double doors.

*

Almost as one, they stopped, dumbfounded by the sight before them.

They had arrived in a high-domed circular chamber some fifty yards across. Thin watery light came in from above where a vaulted ceiling of girders and glass let in sunlight through a layer of thin snow and frost. There were more corpses here, a score of men lying on the floor, almost equally split between civilians in overalls and uniformed airmen. Again, they all appeared to have fallen where they stood, then just gone to sleep and been frozen. Everything was covered in more frost, which felt crisp underfoot. The only sound in the chamber was the crunch as Banks took a step forward, and he winced at the noise, wondering what he would do if any of the dead men woke at that point.

The main thing, the elephant in the room he was trying not to think about, the thing they couldn't drag their eyes from at first, was the silver metal saucer that sat almost exactly in the middle of the chamber. It was twenty yards in diameter, and the only thing breaking the expanse of shining metal was a large red circle at its highest point, with a five-foot-tall, black-on-white Swastika in the center.

The saucer sat flush to the ground, and rose to a maximum height of ten feet at the center of the Swastika. There was no sign of any doorway or window, no method of ingress that Banks could see from where he stood by the doorway.

"Fucking hell," Wiggins said softly, and Banks realized he had nothing of any greater import to add to the statement just then.

*

It took Banks ten seconds to be able to drag his gaze from the saucer. It commanded attention, catching the eye and refusing to let go. The silver surface had avoided all ravages of time – there was none of the otherwise ever-present frost covering the metal, which was polished to a high shine, reflecting the girders and glass roof above in a most disorienting manner that was almost hypnotic.

Finally, Banks looked away, and took in details of the rest of the chamber.

Another bank of the tall metal containers they'd seen in the generator room lined the wall directly to his left. He guessed this was the endpoint of the thicker cable, but as yet couldn't fathom what their purpose was, or what manner of power source might have been in use here.

To his right was obviously the engineering or laboratory

area. A corkboard covered the wall almost a quarter of a way around the outside circle, and it was covered with blueprints, diagrams, and notes. Six long trestle tables were likewise festooned with books, notebooks, and charts.

Banks saw that the rest of the squad was still transfixed by the saucer. He clapped his hands, twice, the noise echoing like a drumbeat in the chamber.

"What's the matter? You lot never seen a fucking Nazi UFO before?" he said. "Parker and Wiggins, find something to stow all this paperwork in. It'll be coming with us when we leave. And take it gently; it's probably going to be fragile."

"I'll imagine it's the sarge's wife," Wiggins said, then had to dodge out of the way to avoid a smack on the head from Hynd.

"Cally, you see if you can make heads or tails of the power system. The rest of you, you're with me," Banks said, and turned his gaze again to the saucer.

*

The first thing he spotted was that the floor area around the saucer was also devoid of frost, to a distance of several yards from the vessel all around. As he got closer, he noticed markings on the floor, what looked like quarter-inch thick lines of gold embedded in the metal plates. Two of the lines appeared to be concentric circles running around the saucer and marking the boundary of the frost-free area. The other marks were a series of straight lines and squiggles that he could make no sense of from a distance.

He stepped forward for a closer look, his left foot landing on the outer of the gold circles. He felt a tingle run through him, not a current surge as such, more like the sensation of licking the poles of a battery. At the same time, a shout rang around the chamber from McCally at the bank of metal containers.

"No, Cap. Back off."

Banks lifted his foot off the circle and stepped away. The

tingling stopped immediately.

"What is it, Cally?" he said.

"Come and see, Cap. I don't have a fucking clue."

Banks walked over to McCally, who stood beside a series of gauges embedded in a panel in the wall. He tapped the top one. It was a meter graded from zero to a number in the millions. The needle pointed at zero.

"This moved," McCally said. "When you took the step forward, it went up. Not by much, but it was noticeable."

Banks shouted across to Hynd who was still at the edge of the outer circle.

"Go on, Sarge," he said. "Just one step, then back again. Don't do anything stupid."

Hynd took a step forward while Banks watched the gauge. There was a small but definite movement of the needle, and it fell back to zero as soon as the sergeant stepped back out of the circle.

"What the hell is this shit, Cap?" McCally said.

"Buggered if I know, Cally. But I don't think we should fuck with it until we've got more intel."

"There's something else, Cap," Hynd said, and motioned that Banks should have a look. The sergeant pointed at his feet as Banks walked over to where he stood. The area of floor that was free of frost had grown, now stretching for an inch beyond the outermost of the gold inlaid circles. Banks bent toward the gold lines and felt heat coming from the circle even before he touched it. It felt warm through his gloves.

"What the fuck, Cap?" Hynd said.

*

Wiggins and Parker returned from the right side of the room. They had managed to find two canvas kit bags, both of which they'd filled with the books, notebooks, and charts that they'd found in the work area.

"Is that the lot?" Banks asked.

Wiggins nodded.

"Everything that was salvageable. The frost had got in too deep to some of the paperwork and it fell apart as soon as we so much as breathed on it. But there's some solid intel in the bags from what we saw while we were packing it."

"Good work," Banks replied then spoke up so that the whole squad could hear him. "I need to call this in, lads. We've got two choices; you can stay underground here in the base, or we set up camp out in the hut with the bunks and the stove."

"I vote we get outside, Cap" Wiggins replied. "This place gives me the screaming heebie-jeebies."

The rest of the squad was in agreement.

"The hut it is then," Banks said. "Let's hope we can get the stove lit; otherwise, it's going to get a tad chilly."

"Maybe we'll just burn Wiggins," Hynd said. "All that lard should keep us toasty for a while."

*

McCally took point again, and now that they knew the route, they made good time through the base and up into the suddenly too-bright Antarctic day. Banks looked straight ahead as they crossed through the open central chamber – he'd seen enough dead for one day. When they reached the top landing, they saw that some of the frost had melted from the man who lay below the main entrance. Some pink showed at his cheek, pink tinged with blue, and Banks again had a vision of the man standing up and going about his day. He stepped quickly over the body, not looking down, wondering whether he'd be able to stifle a scream if a cold hand reached for his ankle. He let out a sigh of relief he didn't realize he'd been holding in when they stepped out into the daylight. He knew it wasn't hot outside, but somehow it felt like a summer day in comparison to the cold, dark bowels of the base's tunnels.

I'm not going back down there again unless I have to.

He closed the door behind him. It shut with a clang that he

hoped was the ringing of a bell to bring the episode to an end.

*

Once they got to the hut, McCally took charge of organizing the men and trying to get the stove going. Banks and Hynd stood in the doorway while Hynd had a smoke.

"I'm going down to the dinghy to call it in, Sarge," Banks said. "If we're lucky, they'll say that the paperwork is enough and we can hightail it back to the boat and a bit of dinner."

"When are we ever lucky?" Hynd replied. "I'll make a start on going through the papers while you're away, just in case."

Banks nodded and left Hynd to his smoke, heading back down the track to the jetty and the dinghy.

In other circumstances, he'd have taken his time and enjoyed the view which was a stunning vista of ice, rock, and clear blue water in picture-postcard quality, but something about this place still had him spooked, and his gut was telling him there was trouble brewing. As he'd told Hynd, he was hoping that the brass back home would be satisfied with the paperwork, but he knew better. As soon as they heard about the saucer, the paperwork would be almost secondary, no matter what revelations lay there.

*

He had to wait while the call was relayed through the icebreaker and on to Whitehall. The clipped tones of the voice at the other end were calm and measured for the most part, but he went quiet at the mention of the saucer, then quieter still when Banks mentioned the two names he'd read – Carnacki and Churchill.

"This needs to go up the chain to the highest level," the man said. "Stay in position, and check back in four hours. We'll have orders for you then."

As he switched off the radio and climbed up out of the

dinghy, Banks already knew what the answer would be. His gut told him, and kept telling him every step back up the track.

- 4 -

At least McCally had managed to get the stove going in the hut, although it was cramped inside with all eight of them in a space that looked to be made for no more than two or three men. Hughes, Patel, and Wilkes sat tight together on the bottom bunk, Wiggins was stretched out on the one above them, Parker and McCally were by the stove, with a kettle on and a pot boiling up some of the thin soup that passed as their rations. They all looked up as Banks entered.

"At ease, lads," he said. "The brass needs some thinking time. Four hours till next check-in, so smoke them if you've got them."

"So what do they think it is, Cap?" Wiggins asked. "Some black ops bullshit cobbled up during the war to try and make us shit ourselves?"

"Aye," Parker said. "I've seen that film. Nazi UFO in a tube station in London, wasn't it? Fucking ace that was."

"This is no black ops," Hynd said, and the room fell quiet. "We all saw the bodies, and the rust on the walls, and the age of the paperwork. It's all too good; in fact, it's fucking perfect. It's exactly what it looks like. No more, no less."

"But, Sarge," Wiggins said. "Fucking NAZI UFOs? That's just sad-sack internet conspiracy theory bollocks."

"Not anymore it isn't," Hynd said. "You saw it. We all saw it."

McCally came over from the stove and put a pot of soup on the table and some bowls and cutlery. The room was already warming up, so much so that Parker and McCally had taken off their outer jackets.

"Get it inside you, lads. We found enough wood to keep the

stove running for a while, so at least we won't freeze our nuts off for the next four hours."

"Turn it down a tad," Banks said. "And eke out the wood as much as you can. We might be here a bit longer than four hours, if my gut's right."

*

Banks and Hynd let the squad get to the soup first. Hynd had been as good as his word and been among the paperwork in the canvas kit bags they'd brought out of the base.

"This all looks legit, Cap," the sergeant said. "But it's as weird as fuck."

"In what way?"

"Well, there's orbital mechanics and flight plans and the like, everything you'd expect if they really were trying to attempt to get that fucker off the ground. But there are all sorts of other bits of shite along with the technical stuff. Take those gold markings on the floor under the saucer, for example. If I'm reading this right, it's a fucking pentagram."

"What, black magic, demonology, all that old bollocks?"

"Exactly. I'd heard the Nazis were mad for that kind of crap, but I never expected to find evidence all the way down here."

"So what next? The fucking Lost Ark?"

Hynd shrugged.

"At this stage, Cap, very little would surprise me."

Banks wasn't really listening to his sergeant. His mind was back in the hangar, his foot on the gold circle, feeling the tingling vibration run through his body. His gut instinct was shouting loud at him now, but he pushed it down.

"Maybe Wiggins was right," he said. "Maybe this is all some kind of black ops psychological shite."

"Aye, maybe," Hynd said. "But what if it isn't?"

Banks clapped Hynd on the shoulder.

"Then we'll just have to kick auld Nick in the nuts and fuck off for a pint," he said. "Like we always do."

*

His attempt at humor seemed to placate the sergeant, but Banks' own mood was sour. After finishing the soup, Hughes, Patel, and Wilkes sat, tight together on the bottom bunk, and all three quickly went to sleep, accompanied by the snoring of Wiggins above them. Banks envied them the rest, but he couldn't get his mind to settle. Parker, McCally, and Hynd got a card game going, but Banks was still thinking of the two names in the journal he'd found, still wondering as to their relevance to the current situation. He stepped over nearer the stove and sat leaning on the counter that served as chopping board and food preparation area. He got the old leather journal from his backpack, opened it up, and continued reading from where he'd left off.

Soon he had left the Antarctic behind, flying back to London, over a hundred years before.

*

I was expecting a parcel of books that Saturday morning, and when the knock came to the door in Cheyne Walk, I almost ran to answer, eagerly anticipating an afternoon of studious endeavor in my library among the pages of some new friends for my shelves. Instead, I found a tall, heavily built lad on my doorstep.

At first glance, I might have taken him for a policeman or a bruiser, for he had something of the manner of both, but his tone was polite, even cultured, as he handed me an envelope.

"I was told to pass this to you personally, sir," he said. "It is for your eyes only."

The envelope was plain, but of expensive paper, and the handwritten note was done most elegantly in the blackest of black inks with not the slightest smudge on it. The wording of the note itself was equally as terse as the deliverer's message.

"I have sent my driver for you. Come immediately. It is of national importance."

I suspected the name even before I read it. It was appended, simply, 'Churchill.' I knew the man well enough from our previous encounters to know he would not be an easy chap to refuse.

I took enough time to fetch an overcoat, a hat, and my pipe and tobacco. The burly young chap stood, stock-still, filling my doorway the whole time, and only moved aside to let me exit. Then I was, if not exactly bundled, enthusiastically encouraged into a waiting carriage and within seconds, we were off and away, heading east at some speed along the Embankment.

I had the interior of the rather well-appointed carriage to myself, the bearer of the telegram having stepped up to sit with the driver. Once we passed Westminster, and didn't stop at Parliament, but continued to head even farther east, I realized it might be a longer trip than I had anticipated.

To pass the time, I read the note again, but it told me nothing new beyond the fact that Churchill was a man who expected to be obeyed. I hadn't heard from him since our last encounter, but I remembered reading of his appointment as First Lord of the Admiralty in The Thunderer *a month or so back. I wondered if this summons might had something to do with that, but I had insufficient facts to hand for such conjecture, and settled for lighting a pipe, trying to enjoy the journey, and not letting my curiosity turn to frayed nerves and a bad temper.*

The carriage kept going along the north side of the river, past St. Paul's and London Bridge, past the Tower, and headed into the warren of old quays and warehouses of the docks. I was starting to regret not having partaken of a larger breakfast.

I was still wondering quite how far I might have to travel when the carriage finally came to a halt at an old boat shed that, once upon a time, must have been one of the largest on the docks. There were a score or more of the young, strapping, silent type of chaps around. Some of them had made some kind of attempt at disguising themselves in old, frayed and worn clothing in an effort to pass themselves off as dockhands. But they weren't fooling me. This was Churchill's work all right, and these were his lads. I guessed they were military, or rather, given Churchill's post, Navy chaps to a man, and they were hard men, trained to kill by the look of them. I decided I had better be on my toes and keep my nose clean as I stepped down from the carriage onto the quay.

*

Churchill was there to meet me. He had grown more stout and portly since our last meeting, and his belly strained rather too tightly against his waistcoat. Compared to his lads around us, he looked out of place on the dock, his walking cane, heavy silver fob chain, tall hat and tails being much too grand, and more suited to the rarified atmosphere of the House.

Given the abrupt nature of my summoning, I half-expected him to be brusque and off-hand. But he was all 'hale fellow, well met' and made a show of telling his lads that I was an expert, consultant I believe is the word he used, and that I was to be given access to the whole site; nothing was to be kept from me. I still had no idea what was kept in the big shed at this point, but at least I knew now that I had been brought for a reason, for Churchill took my arm and suddenly became quite conspiratorial.

*

"It's those bally Huns. They're at it again," he said as he led me toward the large boat shed and to a small door to the rear of the main building. "They're readying for war, I can feel it in my water. And it's my job now to do what I can to stop them mastering the seas. It's our best defense, always has been. But it's also our weakest point, for there are far too many miles of coastline all the way up the North Sea that are undefended and

vulnerable to a sneak attack. We must show that we are prepared for any eventuality. Britannia must rule the waves again, and we must take charge of the oceans now, before it's too late. Don't you agree?"

It had sounded more in the nature of a speech than conversation, so I thought it best to be circumspect and muttered my agreement, to which he clapped me on the shoulder. It appeared we were to be friends, for a while at least.

We came to a halt outside the small door and he turned to me again.

"Now, Carnacki, my good man, I must ask for your complete discretion on this matter. What you are about to see is the best-kept secret in the country at the moment, and we must ensure it remains that way. Apart from my chaps on guard here, there's only ten people know of it. And you are the tenth. The PM knows, but not the cabinet, and not even the King has been told. I know you are a man of your word, so I can trust you to keep this under your hat."

I nodded in reply, but didn't get time to get a word in edgeways as he continued.

"And there are to be no Friday night stories told around the fire over a smoke and a brandy; not with this one. It's too bally sensitive to be bandied about, even between close friends and confidantes. Agreed?"

"Agreed," I replied, although I was feeling increasingly unsure as to what I was letting myself in for. Churchill nodded to the guard beside the door, who opened it to allow us into the cathedral that was the boat shed and reveal Churchill's big secret.

Of all the things I had considered, of all the things I had expected to see, I think a German U-Boat might well have been near the bottom of the list.

*

And yet there it was, like a great russet-colored whale

beached up on timbers that held it off the floor and ran along its whole length. The bulk of it almost filled the old shed from the huge riverside doors to the rear where we stood. I could only look at it in awe, and wonder how it had got here, to the East London docks. Churchill answered my question before I asked it.

"We think she's a prototype for a new class they're developing over there; there's been rumors of such a thing for a year or so now, and it looks like they were right. We caught this one snooping around in the North Sea, up in Doggerland at the shallowest point. Well, we didn't actually catch her. The engineers who've been over her bow to stern tell me that she had some kind of system failure and gave up the ghost all on her own. She was floating on the surface when we got to her, and not a man of the crew left alive inside either. The poor blighters all died of suffocation, or so the doctors assure me."

He paused, and laughed as if he had made a joke.

"Gave up the ghost. That's rather apt, I must remember that one."

He didn't look inclined to explain that point, so I let it lie and went on to the matter that most concerned me.

"So you have a German submarine. That's probably good for you and the Admiralty," I replied. "But I fail to see why you need my particular brand of expertise, or where I am being asked to apply it."

Churchill laughed again, a booming thing that echoed high in the rafters of the shed.

"That is why you would never make a politician or indeed an Admiral, Carnacki. You have failed to see our tactical advantage here, even when it's right in front of your nose."

"I'm still not with you," I replied.

Churchill waved at the length of the submarine in reply.

"It felt like a godsend, when it turned up like that, almost on our doorstep," he said. "A free, no strings attached, chance to examine our largest adversary's latest vessel. But when I looked at it, I started to wonder. It was a simple question at first, but

the implications of it kept making me come back to it again and again.

"What if we gave them it back? What if we gave them it back with something on board that would make them think twice about ever sending something our way again?"

I was starting to see some daylight, and I was wishing that I didn't.

"You want me to mock up some kind of propaganda scene inside the submarine, is that what this is about? I am to make it look like something from beyond killed the crew and that it has been taken over by a spectral presence? Parlor tricks and scare tactics, in other words."

"You've nearly got it, old man," Churchill said, and suddenly he looked completely serious. "But I do not, under any circumstances, want a mere mock-up. There must be no 'parlor tricks' that can be easily exposed as such. I need the real thing. I want this U-boat infested with a particularly vicious spook. I want it sent back to them, and I want to put the fear of God into the bally Hun so that they will never trouble us again."

*

It took a few seconds for all of that to sink in. I did not know whether to be simply confused, or completely appalled. In the end, I pleaded unfit for the task at hand.

"You've seen my methods first-hand, Churchill," I said. "You know my defenses are just that; they are only defensive. I wouldn't know to go about calling up a spook, never mind ensuring you got a nasty, vicious one."

He didn't reply at first; he looked me straight in the eye for the longest time before speaking in a measured voice.

"Come, now. That is not strictly true, is it, Carnacki?" he said finally. "I know for a fact you have a wide variety of books on the shelves in your library dealing with such matters. There must be something in those tomes that is of practical use?"

I did not go into how he might know what I had in my

private library. Just as he had seen my methods first-hand, so I had seen his. He had a ruthless streak in him I found hard to like, and a blatant disregard for any piddling matters such as legality and morality if they did not suit his purposes. He did, however, have the strongest sense of duty to King and Country of any chap I have ever met, and I could not help but be impressed with the zeal with which he approached the task.

But that in itself was not enough to get a job done that I considered to be, frankly, impossible. I tried to tell him so in words he might understand.

"Those are merely books," I said. "It is only research and history. Practically, there is little there of use. Necromancy and demon summoning are only primitive methods of trying to understand the mysteries of the Outer Realms, and I have never encountered a single report that suggests any such attempts were ever successful. Let it go, Churchill. There is no foolproof way of summoning a thing from the Great Beyond, never mind getting one to do your bidding"

"I am not asking for it to be foolproof," Churchill said. "I am only asking for it to be done. Your country needs you, man. Will you refuse it in its hour of need?"

He did not know me well enough to realize that appeals to base patriotism wouldn't wash with me. My country was of little consequence compared to the immensity of the Beyond. But, still, it is my country, and Mr. Churchill is a most persuasive gentleman.

I also had a feeling that if I did refuse him, I might not be making a return journey home from this boat shed. I have seen the shark beneath his smile, and his ruthlessness would not allow his secret to be out and abroad and not under his control. I would have to brazen it out with a brass neck until I could get a clearer idea of how I would need to play it to satisfy his demands.

"What manner of spook do you require?" I asked calmly, as if I knew what I was about.

*

He laughed at that, and hid the shark away. He did not fool me though; I knew it still swam in the depths, waiting to surface when required.

"I knew you were a man of sense," he said. "Come, let's seal our deal over a drink and a smoke and we can discuss it further."

He led me to a small office that was more like a foreman's hut at the back of the shed beyond the submarine propellers. The space was crammed with carpentry tools, blueprints, cameras, and ledgers. And I was not in the least bit surprised to see my box of defenses on the floor amid the clutter, and two tall piles of my books on the table in a space that had obviously been cleared for them. It appeared that Churchill didn't only know the contents of my library; he had the run of the whole bally house.

At least he hadn't needed to have his chaps rifle my liquor cabinet or smokes drawer. He had a tall travelling valise at his side, one of those expensive leather and brass jobs I've had an eye on for myself. He opened it to expose, not books or clothes, but a well-stocked range of liquor in tall decanters, some expensive crystal glasses, and a long wooden cigar box.

He winked at me as he saw my astonishment.

"Perks of the job, old boy," he replied. "One must travel in style, if one must travel at all."

He poured me some rather fine single malt I hadn't had before from Orkney, and passed me a Cuban cigar that was thicker than my thumb and twice as long, before clicking his glass against mine.

"To business," he said after swallowing most of his scotch in a single gulp. I merely sipped at mine. I had a feeling I had a lot of work ahead of me, a feeling that was amplified considerably as he outlined his requirements.

"It has to be strange enough to spook the Huns," he said, "yet not so bloody weird that it'll frighten my men. I'm going to have to have some crew aboard when we take this thing out of here. They'll be needed to get it back into waters where it can be found."

"And what about the original German crewmen? How will their absence be explained?"

"Absence?" Churchill said, and again I saw the ruthless shark under the mask. "Oh, they won't be absent. We have them on ice in a shed not a hundred yards from here. When we're ready, we'll get them back on board and send them off with their boat."

I was less and less keen on this whole business by the second, but I was in too far now to back out.

"I will need to spend some time with my books," I said. "This is not something I can undertake lightly."

Churchill nodded. He poured another large measure of his scotch and topped up mine, although I had as yet scarcely touched it.

"I thought you might say that," he said. "Let me know if you need anything. The chaps outside are at our beck and call at all hours."

He went and sat in the chair across the table opposite me and was immediately lost in his thoughts, a fug of cigar smoke surrounding him like fake ectoplasm at a séance.

It was time for me to get to work.

*

I sipped at the scotch and smoked the cigar as I checked to see what Churchill had thought were the books I might require for the task at hand. Not for the first time, he surprised me with his perspicacity and breadth of knowledge. He had indeed thought of everything, from the Key of Solomon to De Vermis Mysteriis, from several medieval grimoires to my working copy of the Sigsand mss. Of course, as I have said, I considered the bulk of this material to be of historical curiosity value only. I had read them all before, but never with an eye to considering *them as in any way practical.*

I took the time it took me to smoke the cigar to clear my mind of my own preconceptions, and then set about looking for something I thought might have a chance of working, given my talent and expertise, and a large amount of good luck. I had a feeling that I was going to need it.

*

I ploughed through spell after spell, annoyed at myself for agreeing to a course that took me so far from my natural instincts to defend against the very things I was going to attempt to raise. Much of the kind of ritual spellbinding I was perusing is, of course, superstitious mumbo-jumbo; dead men's hands, blood from a pregnant mare, the skull of a dog killed at a crossroads; all stuff and nonsense. And besides, procuring any such items in time for Churchill's purposes was going to prove problematic, to say the least. I aimed for something that might be simple, but effective, which proved to be another problem; the old coves responsible for writing these things didn't really go in for doing anything the easy way.

But finally I settled on something I found in 'The Mysteries of the Worm,' a binding spell for summoning a hellish entity that could cloud men's minds and make them go mad at the sight of it. It sounded like the kind of thing that Churchill might be after, and even if it didn't work, I had the passage right there in the book to point at, to show him that I'd at least tried.

I was, however, not quite stupid enough to walk directly into a dark place and start chanting a centuries-old demon summoning ritual. I would need some protection. I got up to check that nothing in my box of defenses had been damaged in its journey here.

Churchill looked up as I opened the box.

"Another snifter?" he said, and raised his empty glass.

"No," I replied. 'But I shall definitely need one when I return. I think I've found what you asked for."

"And will it work?"
"We shall know one way or another in a couple of hours."

*

It was mid-afternoon and already starting to get rather dim inside the big boat shed as I carried my box of defenses up the makeshift gangway that led to the flat, main deck of the submarine. My footsteps clanged on metal and echoed, hollow, like funeral bells, all around me. The chill I immediately felt in my spine did not bode well for my state of mind to deal with what was coming next.

I considered setting up on that open, flat surface, but Churchill would want this job done properly. I would have to descend into the bowels of the beast so to speak. That was easier said than done, for there were no obvious exterior hatches. To get inside, I had to manhandle the bally box up the railed steps of the turret, and back down the other side once I got inside. As a result, I was dashed hot and bothered before I even started to investigate the interior of the vessel.

I had enough light coming in from above me to open my box and get out the small oil lantern I carry within it. I lit it up and started to look for somewhere I could set up my circles.

It was immediately obvious that I was going to have some difficulty. Conditions were cramped inside the submarine, to say the least, and there appeared to be no single spot of floor large enough to contain my defenses. The air inside the vessel felt heavy and slightly warm; it stank, of burnt oil and stale breath. To my left was a tall and wide bank of meters and dials I could make no sense of whatsoever, and to my right long lines of piping and wiring stretched off in both directions down the dark corridors. There was no sound save any that I was making, and even the tiniest movement, the merest scrape of sole on deck, was amplified in whispering echoes that ran up and down the length of the boat.

My lamp did not penetrate far into the darkness, and I was

suddenly all too aware of Churchill's tale of the thirty dead crewmen who had met their end, locked in this metal box under who knows how many feet of cold water. That made my mind up for me. I could possibly have spent more time searching for a better, wider, spot, but now that I was here, I wanted to get things done as quickly as possible and get back to the bottle of scotch and some living company.

As I have said, I was in a tight spot. So I improvised. I stood in the main control area, which was slightly toward the bow under the turret, and set up a pair of small circles in chalk that were as wide as I could make them in the space I had available. Then I transcribed the pentagram, noticing that there was now only just, by a matter of inches, enough space for me to stand with my feet together inside the defenses. That, obviously, meant that my valves for the pentacle were much closer together than I would have liked, with only the span of a hand separating them, but I managed to quickly get them aligned in the peaks and troughs of the pentagram, and switched on the battery pack.

The resultant hum echoed and thrummed through the whole bally vessel, and a wave of cold rushed through the corridors, a cold, damp, breeze as if a heavy fog had descended. My heart thudded faster, and my knees went to jelly before I remembered that I had stood in worse bally spots than this, facing real danger, not imagined spooks. I berated myself for letting the dark and Churchill's story get to me.

I stepped into the defenses, lit a pipe, and composed myself.

It was time to begin.

*

I will not reproduce the spell that I used here. Even inadvertent reading of these old incantations is thought by practitioners to cause unforeseen and unwanted effects, so it is probably for the best not to tempt fate. Besides, I did not get the opportunity to finish even the first stanza of the chant.

A great wall of darkness rushed at me out of the aft

corridor, and all of the valves of the pentacle flared at once, so bright I was forced to close my eyes against the sudden brilliance. I heard the valves whine, and felt again the wave of cold and damp wash over and around me. I tasted salt spray at my lips.

When I opened my eyes again, I thought the brightness had temporarily caused a problem with my sight, for although I stood inside the shining pentacle, and color washed over and around me, there was nothing but black velvet dark beyond the boundaries of my circles.

I felt the weight of the darkness press against the pentacle, as if something solid were testing itself against the defenses. Cold seeped up from the deck, gripping at my ankles and calves as if I stood in a deep puddle of freezing water, and my teeth started to chatter until I clamped them down on the stem of my pipe.

The valves pulsed and whined and the green one in particular was under a deal of strain. The darkness got darker, the cold got colder, and I felt something in my mind, a searching, questing thought, as if the dark was looking for a way inside. I knew I had to resist. I could not succumb, for if I did I would never leave this vessel alive.

I started to recite an old Gaelic protection prayer that had proved efficacious for me in the past, mumbling through my clenched teeth, focussing all my attention on the words.

The darkness continued to press, hard, against all of my defenses. I struggled for breath, felt coldness pour down my throat, salty again, like the sea, and the dark swelled and closed in even tighter.

I summoned up all the strength I had in me and continued the Gaelic right through to its end. I called out the last words.

Dhumna Ort!

The blue valve blazed at my last shout, and all at once the blackness washed away, so suddenly it might never have been there at all. I stood there as the pentacle valves dimmed to a normal level and blood started to pump faster in my veins,

warming parts that had been in danger of being frozen.
I had no need to call up one of Churchill's favored spooks.
There appeared to be one on board already.

- 5 -

Banks stopped reading and shut the journal with a snap that caused Hynd to look up from his cards and raise an eyebrow.

"More fucking demonology bollocks and shite," Banks said with a grim smile. The sarge went back to the card game, but Banks sat by the stove, staring into space. He didn't believe his own oaths. It hadn't read like *bollocks and shite*. And that was the problem. It had read like cold, hard fact, and he believed every word of it to be true. He still didn't see how it applied to their situation here. But he was afraid he was getting closer to an answer, one that he wasn't going to like.

The card game was still going strong, but Banks wasn't in the mood to join in– besides, he usually lost to the men, either through bad play on his part, or by design to help morale. What he really needed was a stiff drink to settle his gut down, but the nearest scotch was back on the boat, and well out of reach. Instead, he made for the kit bags and began rummaging through the heap of books, notebooks, and papers that had been collected in the hangar room.

It looked like everything was in German apart from the journal he'd lifted from the oberst's desk. He ploughed through a thick log book of the base operations, looking for clues as to their fate, reading list after list of supply deliveries, personnel coming and going. The fuel consumption figure in particular caught his eye – it was remarkably low, consider the German's had been on site for many months. He was looking for clues as to what had befallen the base, but there was nothing in the logbook to suggest an oncoming calamity.

He moved on to what appeared to be the oberst's personal journal, and an ongoing record of the saucer's construction. The name Carnacki was obvious in places among the German, but Banks' grasp of the language wasn't sufficient to the task of deciphering it enough to get any kind of understanding.

He moved on to the diagrams and charts. The blueprints looked remarkably simple, far too simple for something that purported to be a space-going vehicle, and Banks started to wonder if the black-ops propaganda theory might not be the closest to reality. Then he came upon a package wrapped in thick waxed paper. Inside was a series of several dozen black and white photographs.

The first showed two airmen in heated flight suits. They looked alike enough to be twins, young and sturdy, clean-cut blond men with fresh-faced smiles, standing in the hangar with the shining silver shell of the saucer behind them. The second showed the saucer itself, sitting in the center of the hangar, and although there was no color, the lines and circles on the floor beneath it were definitely glowing, looking brilliant white in the photograph. The third photograph showed the two men inside the saucer, which appeared to be almost an empty shell. Banks got a shiver to see that the men appeared to be standing inside individual pentagrams, reminding him all too clearly of what he'd been reading in the Carnacki journal.

But it was the fourth photograph that caught his breath in his throat and demolished the black ops theory once and for all. Although it was black and white, and very grainy compared to modern photographic methods, the image was clear enough. It was a coastline Banks couldn't identify, but taken from such a height that there could be no doubt, especially after a quick glance through the rest of the photographs in his hands that showed more pictures taken from a great height. The saucer had made a flight. More than that, it had made it into orbit.

He turned the last photograph over. There was a black swastika stamped in ink on it, and a date. It matched the date he'd seen circled in red on the oberst's wall calendar – the 4th of January, 1942.

*

Now that he'd seen the pilots standing in the pentagrams, Banks knew he needed to finish the Carnacki journal. It was too important to be ignored, indeed might be the pivotal key required for understanding the whole matter. He went back to the stove, and back to the journal, trying to quell the growing dissatisfaction in his gut.

He took up again exactly where he'd left off.

*

Now that the darkness had washed away, and I could no longer feel any presence, every part of me wanted to step out of the circles and head up and out into warmer air, and a place where there was a large glass of good scotch waiting for me. But I knew Churchill's mind. He would want to know more of the nature of this new thing I had found, and how it could be pressed to become an advantage in his favor. And to do that, I would have to face the thing again.

I stood still and lit a fresh pipe. The taste of tobacco did much to remind me that I wasn't lost down here in the dark, that I was here of my own free will. I was here to learn.

The gray fug of smoke wafted away through the corridors of the vessel. My valves lit up enough of the corridors in front and behind of me to show that there was no sign of the wall of darkness. I knew, of course, that the thing had not simply departed, for it is my experience that once an entity of the Outer Darkness arrives on this plane, they settle, and they are slow to leave.

I was proved right minutes later when the darkness gathered again in the forward corridor. As if it was aware of my presence now, it crept much more slowly than before. And as it was aware of me, so too, I was aware of it. It was less menacing this time, now that I knew it was there.

As before, the blackness gathered around the edges of my

defensive circles, testing the boundaries of the valves; first the yellow one then the green flared and dimmed, flared and dimmed. Once again, cold seeped into my lower limbs and damp air washed against me.

I knew what was coming next. This time, when the darkness sent out its dark probe to my mind, I grabbed hold of it and followed it back to the source, a mental projection trick that let me glimpse, however briefly, some of the thing's innate nature and intent. Fragments of what passed for its thoughts came to me, like images in my mind.

It was old, old and cold, and lost. It had slept for aeons in a deep place in the sea, undisturbed by storm or ice, lying, slumbering in the weed and stone, having been imprisoned even before the sea washed over it for the first time. Men had caught it, men wearing animal furs and wielding stone axes, wooden shields, and long-forgotten ways of dealing with visitors from the Outer Darkness.

And so, it had slept, and dreamed for the longest time. And then, after an age of cold, dank, dark, an iron thing came swimming in the waters above, breaking ancient bonds that the German submariners never even knew existed, allowing the darkness to surge and flow and fill them up.

I felt those poor German lads die, as if I had been the dark thing in the dark, and sudden, unbidden tears filled my eyes, and guilt hit me, hard. That broke my concentration, and alerted the dark to my presence.

It pushed against me hard, the shock almost sending me reeling outside the circles. The green valve flared and I thought I saw, for an instant, an even darker mass of blackness in the shadows, an amorphous, shifting, thing that spoke a word in a language that I did not know but guessed the intent. There was only one thing this darkness wanted.

Home.

*

I spoke the Gaelic words again, and as before the blackness faded away, retreating down the corridors to wherever it was hiding itself in the bowels. This time, I did not delay. I stepped out of the circles, left the pentacle on the deck, and made my way quickly up the turret ladder, out to the boat shed above, then, almost running, down the gangway and into the foreman's office, where I headed straight for the scotch.

Churchill was sipping at a glass of his own and puffing on another cigar. He raised an eyebrow and smiled thinly.

"I gather from your rather startled demeanor that you have had some success?"

I downed a couple of fingers and waited until it hit my stomach and spread its heat before answering.

"I had some failure, and some of what you might regard as success. Although I am not convinced that success is the proper word for what I have experienced."

He sat me down and joined me in another drink. He tried to ply me with another of his, frankly, enormous cigars, but I preferred the pipe. I puffed hard at it as I spoke, and he listened to my tale, without even the slightest hint of incredulity. He went quiet and thought for a few seconds before he spoke softly.

"So this thing in the dark that you saw? You believe it is what killed the Hun crew?"

"I believe so," I replied. "In fact, I am sure of it."

"I would like to see it for myself," he said.

I protested long and hard at that, but his final answer was what persuaded me.

"I will not ask my men to do something I would not do myself," he said, and by Jove, I think he meant it.

*

I went back with him as far as the deck of the submarine, but he bade me stand outside.

"As you did yourself, I will face this thing alone, in the same way as the men will have to face it to perform the task I must set for them."

I warned him to step over the circles into the inside of the pentacle, and not to break the protection once he was inside, no matter what might happen. I also gave him the last two words of the Gaelic chant, as a last resort should they be needed.

"Wish me luck, old chap," he said as he turned away. "I have faced many battles, but I do believe this short walk might be among the hardest things I shall be called to do for my country."

I agreed with him on that, but he went anyway. He was still chewing down hard on that infernal cigar as he climbed up and over, into the turret and down into the bowels of the sub.

I stood there for long minutes, straining to hear, waiting for a cry for help and ready to go to his aid if needed. For the longest time, there was no sound save my own breathing and the slight hiss of burning tobacco in my pipe. Then, as if from a great distance, I heard it, a voice raised in a shout, the old Gaelic phrase repeated twice. It sounded as if the second time contained more than a trace of fear.

Dhumna Ort! Dhumna Ort!

I had started climbing up the turret when I heard scrambling sounds above me, and had to retreat as Churchill descended out of the sub with some haste. He did not stop to acknowledge me, but marched, almost running, away along the deck and down the gangway. By the time I reached the foreman's office, he was already making impressive headway down the scotch, gulping it down unceremoniously straight from the neck of the decanter.

He only spoke when he came up for air. His cheeks were now ruddy, but he was pale around the lips, with dark shadows under his eyes, and his hands shook badly as he lit a fresh cigar.

"That dashed thing killed the Huns," he said, and this time it wasn't a question.

But if I thought his experience might mean a change in course for his plan of action and a softening of his resolve, I was to be proved wrong with his next sentence.

"Can you show someone how to make that pentacle of yours? We will need one for each of the men. I shudder to think what might have happened had I not been inside it."

*

I spent the night sitting in that cramped little room, drinking and smoking with Churchill. Every so often, he would call for one or another of his men and bark an order at them. But mostly we talked, of inconsequential matters; he spoke with some elegance, and not a little sense of regret, of his time as a journalist, and I regaled him with some of the tales that my friend Dodgson has already detailed in his journals. At some point I slept, and when I woke, Churchill was gone and about his business for King and Country.

As for myself, I never set foot inside the sub again after I retrieved my box of defenses the next morning. I spent two more days at the boat shed instructing Churchill's men in the art of pentacle defense, and showed some Naval engineers the trick of the valves and wires needed for their construction.

*

I heard no more for a week, then out of the blue, I received another summons to the dockyard late of a Sunday evening.

The river was as quiet as it gets, and there was no ceremony. Firstly, they loaded the dead Germans. I did not watch that part, for I was reminded all too vividly of the impressions I had received of their passing from the thing in the cold wet dark. I stood in the shed doorway, smoking a pipe until that part of the job was done.

Then fifteen of Churchill's men went on board, each carrying a small bag of luggage and a box that closely resembled my own box of defenses. Churchill had a word and a handshake for every one of them, but if he had any qualms about what he was doing, they did not show.

Churchill and I retired to the hut at the rear again, where we shared more of his fine scotch until, almost an hour later, the big shed doors were opened, the timber wedges were knocked away and the sub slid, almost silently into the river.

We went out onto the dock to watch it head off out toward the Estuary, a great dark shark cruising on the still waters.

"I don't know about the Germans," I said, "but it certainly scares me."

"They will take her out into the North Sea and leave her floating as near to where we found her as they can manage," Churchill said. "Hopefully, the Huns will find her before the sea claims her again."

"And your men? How will they return?"

Churchill looked at me, and now, for the first time, I saw how deeply he had been affected. He had fresh tears in his eyes.

"They have their orders," he said, turned his back on me, and walked away.

I never heard of the fate of the submarine, or Churchill's men, and although I have met Churchill twice since, he has never spoken of it.

But some nights, when the fog rolls in from the river and I smell salt in the air, I dream of them cruising along in the deep dark, all dead at their posts while the cold blackness swirls around them.

I hope it was worth it.

*

Banks closed the journal softly this time, lost in thought, feeling the pieces of the jigsaw click together as he processed the information he'd just read.

The Germans had indeed found the sub after Churchill had it returned. But far from it scaring them, or perhaps despite it scaring them, they had turned it back to their advantage, somehow taming the thing Carnacki had found in the sub, and molding it to their own devices. It was no great surprise, given their corruption of everything they ever touched, and it seemed impossibly outlandish, but Banks had seen all the evidence now, and could come to no other conclusion.

They got the idea from Winston bloody Churchill.
They used a fucking demon to power a UFO.

- 6 -

He thought it was a bombshell that would cause a ruction back in Whitehall and was prepared for a sense of urgency, or even official denial and an immediate cover-up. But when he went back to the dinghy for his checkpoint call after four hours, the voice at the other end listened to his report and answered only in the same calm, measured, voice.

"Secure and sanitize the base," the man said after Banks had told him everything. "We're sending a team down to relieve you, but it might be a day until we can round them all up and deliver them. In the meantime, find out everything you can that you think might be relevant. Hold out there and keep your heads down."

Secure and sanitize. The squad's not going to like that.

*

"What do you mean, they flew it?" Wiggins said. Banks had the team assembled, standing in a line in the hut, and had just brought them up to speed on his reading. "Surely somebody would have spotted a big shiny bugger of a thing like that in orbit?"

"It was 1942, lad," Banks replied. "Everybody was a wee bit busy either shooting or getting shot at."

"It's not that big a stretch though," Hynd added. "Von Braun was a fucking genius by all accounts. And there's long been rumors about other stuff the Yanks have hidden away in their desert bunkers."

"Aye," McCally said. "But yon was wee green alien buddies from Roswell. Not fucking demons from the North

Sea."

Banks put a hand up to stop the conjecture.

"We've got our orders, and that's all we need to know. Secure and sanitize."

"Aye, about that, Cap," Wiggins said. "You mean moving the bodies, don't you? Do we get time and a half for that shite?"

"You get a skelp on the arse for cheek," Hynd butted in, but Banks just smiled.

"I'll stand for a couple of rounds once we get back to the boat. But for now, we've got our orders. It's cleaning up time, so let's get to it."

*

Wiggins took point going up the slope toward the concealed base entrance.

"We'll drag them all up into the open and stack them in the huts," Banks said. "I'd prefer to burn them, but the team that's coming in will want to see them close up. We'll start with the one in the stairwell to clear the passageway. Parker, you're with Wiggins. The sooner we get this done, the sooner we can get back for a heat and a brew."

The two men opened up the metal hatch, sending a shrieking squeal across the bay, then went down into the darkness. Banks expected them to return with a body, but Wiggins came back alone, and only had his rifle in his hands.

"You need to see this, Cap,"

"Is there a problem with the body?"

"You could say that," Wiggins replied. "The bastard thing has buggered off."

Banks went down into the dark. The first thing he saw was Parker's too-pale face staring back up at him. The man stood on the landing where they'd found the first body, but the private was the only person now in sight. The floor underfoot was too messed with the squad's footprints to make anything out in the frost – the only thing that was obvious was that the body no long lay there.

"Okay, lads, you've had your fun. Where the fuck's the Jerry?"

But he knew as soon as he said it that this was no joke – he saw the confusion in Parker's face, and not a little fear.

"Well, the fucker didn't get up and walk," Banks said. "He was about the stiffest stiff I've ever seen. And he didn't get brought out the hatch – we'd have heard the squeal, even above Wiggins' bloody snoring. So he has to be down there in the hole somewhere. Somebody's yanking our chains here, lads. Let's go and sort them out."

*

Banks led the team back into the bowels of the base. He didn't have to reach the foot of the stairwell to the first chamber to know that something had changed. He felt it, a subtle feeling that someone had been moving around in their absence. What had been dead and empty before was now somehow alive, and the feeling of being watched, measured, was impossible to ignore. It became even more so when they stepped off the bottom rung into the central living chamber of the base.

"What the fuck, Cap?" Hynd said at his side.

The chamber was empty. Where before there had been bodies lying everywhere, now there was only open floor space. It was still impossible to tell anything from the mass of footprints and scrapes they'd left in the frost earlier, but Banks thought there were more prints now, as if the dead had got up and walked away.

Away to where?

The squad assembled at the foot of the stairs, none of them wanting to venture any farther into the large empty chamber.

Get them moving. Get yourself moving.

"Same teams as before," he said, and was pleased there was no tremor in his voice. "Cally, take your lads right, we'll go left, and meet at the double doors. Any trouble, shoot first and we'll sort it out later. Any questions?"

Of course there were questions, but the squad kept them all to themselves. All banter was forgotten now; without needing to be told they'd, as one, gone to battle readiness. Banks felt the same steel firm inside him. He'd faced trouble before and was ready for anything that came his way.

He led Hynd, Parker, and Wiggins to the leftward semi-circle of rooms and sleeping quarters.

*

The rooms were now empty and devoid even of the corpses of the frozen dead. And now it really was noticeable that they'd moved, or been moved, for there were two rooms they hadn't bothered entering on their last visit, and both now had fresh footprints on the floor, leading from the bunk beds to the door and out into the chamber.

"I don't like this shite, Cap," Wiggins said.

"Nor me, lad. But we've still got a job to do here. And I'm not ready to believe they got up and walked, not unless we've missed the Second Coming. They're around here somewhere. They have to be."

But there were no bodies to be found in any of the rooms, nor in the kitchen and mess area, which was as quiet as the first time they'd looked inside. The generator room was likewise empty, but when Banks put a hand on the metal cube of the generator itself he thought, just for a moment, that he felt a faint vibration. He couldn't repeat it though – the next time he put out a hand, he felt only cold metal. In the oberst's office, the chair in which the man had sat was overturned, as if the occupant had stood too hastily to leave.

They met McCally and the other team at the double doors. McCally spoke first.

"Nothing doing, Cap. It looks like they all just got up and walked away."

"Aye, same over here," Banks replied. "This is some fucked

up shite right enough. If it's a joke, I'm not laughing."

He looked at the double door ahead of them.

"There's only one place they can be. Heads up, lads, we're going in hard and fast."

- 7 -

They all felt it as soon as they opened the double door, a breath of air, warm air, coming from up the corridor. There was no accompanying smell, no hint of either fresh air or of death, but Banks' gut had started to grumble at him again, and he knew the cause of it this time.

Whatever's happening, that bloody saucer is at the center of it.

The squad moved forward as one. Banks sensed their alertness, their readiness to face anything that put itself in their path. It's what they trained for, why they had been selected for this unit; to a man, they had the ability to face down danger without fear and fight back until they couldn't fight any longer. He'd trust any one of them with his life.

But what if there's nothing here for us to fight?

He pushed the thought away, focusing only on the here and now as they went quickly along the corridor. It got noticeably warmer the farther they went. Light showed in the windows of the door leading to the saucer hangar, and Banks judged that it was now brighter inside than on their last visit.

"Steady, lads," he whispered, and they made the next ten steps in silence. He stopped the squad at the door. He didn't speak, but motioned to Hynd that he should take McCally and the three others to the left, while he, Wiggins, and Parker went right.

Then he pushed open the door.

*

The air was much warmer now – Banks felt heat wash on

his cheeks and brow. And the cause was immediately obvious. The golden circles and lines that circled the saucer on the floor glowed golden, a radiating heat as warm as the bar on any electric fire. The silver surface of the saucer caught the glow and reflected it back, somehow adding to the sense of a radiator that was in the process of warming up even farther.

High above the saucer, white fluffy clouds scudded across blue sky that showed through the domed glass roof – the snow and frost beyond the glass had already melted away, as it had on the floor, where the damp patch now stretched almost to the doorway where they stood. Small streams of water ran down the walls from condensed drips of melting frost, the only movement in the hangar apart from themselves.

Banks had been convinced that the corpses of the dead must have been brought into this area – they had searched everywhere else there was to search in the facility – but the larger chamber was empty – the corpses that had been on the floor were gone from here too. The hangar did not, however, feel empty – it felt that the saucer watched them, a huge, unblinking, eye. Again, Banks' gut told him they were being scrutinized by something that was gauging them, measuring the risk they posed.

Wiggins called from his right.

"Cap, you need to see this."

Banks went over to where the private stood by the meters and gauges along the wall. The meter that had been down at zero on their last visit now hovered at a reading in the hundreds, and was definitely rising, albeit slowly.

"What the fuck is this shite, Cap?" Wiggins asked, but Banks didn't have an answer for him. He didn't have an answer for much of anything.

*

Hynd brought the rest of the squad back to join the others when it was obvious there was no sign of either the dead, or of any immediate threat, in the hangar.

"Somebody's definitely screwing with us here," Wiggins said.

"You think?" McCally replied. "It's like a fucking bad horror movie."

"Nah. I don't see any lasses with huge knockers hanging out of their dresses."

"Yet," McCally replied.

"Stow that shite, lads. We're on the clock here. So what now, Cap?" Hynd asked.

Banks looked back at the saucer. It seemed even more golden now. The glow from the floor markings was definitely intensifying, and the meter still rose.

If it's this warm when the meter is only at the low levels, what the blazes will it be like when it gets fully charged?

He pushed the speculation away; he didn't have enough information to form any conclusions – at least none that made any sense to him. He turned away from the gauges to talk to the sergeant.

"There's only one other place those bodies could be," he replied, and looked over the sarge's shoulder at the still unblinking golden eye of the saucer.

Hynd saw where Banks was looking.

"In there? Don't talk bollocks, Cap. There's not enough room."

Banks let out a harsh laugh.

"Maybe it's bigger on the fucking inside."

"Aye," Hynd replied. "That's all we need right now, fucking Daleks."

"Can you see a door?" Wiggins said. "I cannae see any door in the bloody thing. How the fuck do we get inside?"

"If you're so bloody keen, lad, then come with me and we'll find out," Banks said. He turned back to Hynd. "Watch the doors, and watch our backs. Any funny business, shout loud and we'll get the fuck out of there fast. Understood?"

Nobody asked what he meant by 'funny business,' and he was glad of that, for he wasn't quite sure himself. He only knew what his gut was telling him – shouting at him now – but he forced himself to take a step toward the saucer, then another.

Wiggins followed him, two steps behind.

*

Banks stopped when he reached the outer gold circle. He unzipped his parka and dropped back the hood – it was several degrees warmer again this close to the source of the heat, and he felt it rise in waves from the golden circles on the floor.

"Fucking Nazi under-floor heating," Wiggins said. "The bastards thought of everything."

Banks put a finger to his lips, and Wiggins went quiet. Across the chamber at the door, the rest of the squad stood watching them, apart from McCally, who'd gone over to watch the gauges and meters.

Banks stepped over the two concentric outer gold rings, but didn't move inside yet, straddling the gold circles with a foot on either side. McCally immediately called out.

"The meter's rising faster, Cap,"

"I thought it might," Banks called back. "Something's responding to our presence here. I think we've started something up. So if anything starts happening apart from the meter moving, shout. And shout loud, okay?"

McCally gave him an okay sign, and Banks stepped all the way inside the circles, taking care not to tread on any of the other golden lines and squiggles. He braced himself, not knowing if an attack was coming but prepared for one anyway, but there was only the steadily rising heat, with no indication that his presence in the circles had been noted in any way.

It was as warm as any British summer's day now, the heat rising upward, like sun off hot sand at a beach, but Banks refused to shuck off his cold weather jacket – he had no guarantee that this warmth wouldn't disappear as quickly as it had started.

He motioned to the private, and Wiggins stepped gingerly

over the gold circles to join him. This †
note. As soon as the man was fully insi‹
then a creak echoed across the hangar, a‹
the saucer, it was to see a door-shaped ‹
to their left ahead of them.

"Little pigs, little pigs, let me come ın,
as Banks stepped forward.

*

Banks took off his gloves, unzipped his outer jacket, and
stepped right up close to the saucer. He put a hand on what he
hoped was the doorway. He'd expected the metal to be warm to
the touch, but it felt cold, almost bitterly so, under his fingers.

He turned back to look at McCally. The corporal made a
maybe yes, maybe no motion with his left hand. That wasn't
enough to stay Banks from his chosen course of action. He
pushed on the metal, and it gave way under the pressure, sinking
several inches inward before sliding aside to his right with a
squealing creak that spoke of a mechanism that had not been
used for many years.

Beyond the revealed entrance, the interior of the saucer lay
in darkness and a cold breath of winter came out, accompanied
by the smell of stale air and dust. There was still no hint of the
stench of death, and Banks took that as a good sign. He pulled
down his night-vision goggles and stepped up inside the craft.

*

The floor was cold underfoot. He felt it rise through the
heavy rubber soles of his boots, and through the material of his
trousers at his ankles and shins, feeling colder still after the
relative warmth just feet away outside the door. He tensed,
ready for action should any of the shifting shadows look to be
getting closer to him, but there were no bodies inside the vessel,
no life of any kind. Even more surprisingly, instrumentation,

mechanisms or means of propulsion, were all noticeable by their absence – the saucer was little more than an empty hell of metal only an inch or so thick. Only a long window on the opposite side from the doorway broke the monotony of the blank walls. Despite the age that the documentation had intimated, there was no sign of any rust or degradation of the metal inside the saucer, and if he hadn't known better, Banks might have thought the whole structure newly built sometime not long before they arrived.

As he stepped inside farther, the window across the saucer was letting in enough light that he could abandon the night goggles again and look around properly. Despite the rising heat out in the hangar, the floor and walls of the interior of the saucer had a thin covering of frost, and the cold was severe enough for Banks to zip up his parka again and pull the hood up over his ears.

There were no footprints on the floor save his own leading in from the doorway, and no sign that anyone had entered the vessel in the years since it had taken its position on the hangar floor. There was certainly no sign that the bodies of the dead had ever been stacked inside at any time, never mind in the past few hours.

And yet his gut shouted at him even louder now. Something was definitely off here, and it had him twitching. He almost jumped when Wiggins spoke behind him.

"Is it safe to come up inside, Cap?"

Banks motioned the other man forward, but stopped him from going further than he had gone himself. He heard his own confusion echoed back at him when Wiggins spoke again.

"What the fuck is this, Cap? Surely this bugger never went anywhere? There's no fucking controls."

Banks hushed the younger man to silence – he'd spotted something else, and as he moved across the saucer floor toward the window, his heart sank to see what was inlaid on the floor. There were more of the golden circles and lines here, two sets of them, twin pentacles set on the floor six feet apart and eight feet from the window, the same ones he'd seen the young blond pilots stand inside in the photographs.

As Banks approached the left side one, the lines took on a dim glow, and the frost melted around the outer circle. Dark shadows swirled around the interior of the craft, and Banks tasted an impossibility: salt water, ice-cold at his lips. He heard a whisper, soft and low, like air escaping from a tire.

"Do you hear that, Cap?" Wiggins whispered.

Banks nodded and put a finger to his lips again, calling for quiet. The sibilant sound echoed around the saucer interior, melding with the rise of distant chanting, a choir singing in a wind. Banks couldn't pinpoint any source. If it was a recording, there was no obvious mechanism, and no off switch. And whatever it was, it was getting steadily louder.

"Where the fuck is it coming from?" Wiggins whispered, as if suddenly afraid to raise his voice. The chanting got closer, a strange, guttural cacophony that contained no words of any language Banks could recognize. At that point, he wasn't even sure that human vocal chords were capable of making the sounds he heard, yips and cries, chirps and whistles intermingled with bass drones and harsh glottal stops. The whole effect was exaggerated by a sudden blast of even colder air that swept through the saucer like a gale.

"Somebody opened a window," Wiggins said.

"I don't think so," Banks replied, and pointed at a spot between the two pentacles on the floor.

At first, it was just a darker shadow that sucked the light away, leaving only bitter cold behind. Banks strained to make out detail as the chanting rang in his ears and the floor of the saucer vibrated in sympathy, swaying lazily in time. A shout came from outside, McCally by the sound of it, but he was so very far away, and Banks couldn't drag his gaze away from the dancing shadow between the pentacles on the floor.

The chanting took on a definite beat that set his whole body shaking, vibrating with the rhythm. Flakes of frosty ice tumbled from the walls, the sound as they hit the floor also, impossibly, in perfect time with the growing beat. Banks' head swam, an effect not dissimilar to knocking back a large measure of liquor too quickly, and it seemed as if the walls of the saucer melted and ran, as if they too were made of no more than melting frost and ice. The light from the window receded into a great distance until it was little more than a pinpoint in a blanket of darkness, and Banks was left alone, in a cathedral of emptiness where nothing existed save the dark and the pounding chant.

He saw stars, in vast swathes of gold and blue and silver, all dancing in great purple and red clouds that spun webs of grandeur across unending vistas. Shapes moved in and among the nebulae; impossibly huge, dark, wispy shadows casting a pallor over whole galaxies at a time, shadows that capered and whirled as the dance grew ever more frenetic. Banks was buffeted, as if by a strong, surging tide, and tasted salt water at his lips again, but as the beat grew ever stronger, he cared little. He gave himself to it, lost in the dance, lost in the stars.

He didn't know how long he wandered in the space between. He forgot himself, forgot Wiggins, dancing in the vastness where only rhythm mattered.

Lost in the dance.

*

He only came out of it slowly, aware that someone was shouting in his face. The voice sounded alien and strange, and it was a struggle to even recognize the noise as words at first, for they echoed and boomed, coming from a great distance down a long tunnel.

"Cap? John? Come on, man, wake the fuck up."

Banks finally found something to grab on to. John – that was his name, somewhere that wasn't out in the dark, somewhere firm, somewhere he had a friend. He mouthed a word, trying it out for size in his throat, then managed a whisper.

"Hynd?"

"Aye, it's me, man. Come on, Cap. Come back to us."

The chanting receded as fast as it had come, and Banks' sight returned between one blink and the next. He looked up to see his sergeant lean over him. Hynd had a concerned look on his face. At the same moment Banks noticed that fact, he also realized that he could see the high glass dome of the hangar roof over the sergeant's shoulder.

"What the fuck am I doing on the floor?"

Hynd laughed bitterly.

"I was going to ask you the same thing. Cally and I had to drag you and Wiggins out of yon fucking saucer. We found you both lying on the floor, twitching and singing to yourselves. It's as if you were hypnotized or something."

"Aye, or something," Banks said, and tried to stand, only to find that he had gone dizzy and weak at the knees. Hynd had to help him upright. He noticed that he'd been dragged all the way out of the saucer, and all the way out of the glowing golden circles, and was now standing over nearby the gauges and meters.

He turned to look at the saucer, then wondered if he had come all the way out of the dream after all. Where before it had sat flush to the floor, the craft now hovered, six inches clear of the lines of the pentagram. There was no sign of the door again, just a seamless stretch of smooth metal. The craft hung in the air, golden yellow now, and humming softly.

We turned the fucker on.

- 8 -

Banks' head cleared slowly, enough for him to be aware that the squad was all looking to him for direction. This was beyond their training – beyond Banks' training too – there was nothing here to fight, nothing to shoot, just the golden hovering craft, six inches off the floor with no sign of any controls or engines to indicate how it was done, its sheer impossibility taunting them.

"It's a trick; it has to be," McCally said.

"It's a fucking great trick though," Wiggins said. He too was looking groggy, but he pushed McCally away when the corporal offered a helping hand. "Under the floor heating, disappearing dead men, and now the grand finale, the incredible levitating UFO. Fucking Nazi wankers are really taking the piss now."

Banks saw that he was within seconds of losing the squad's attention completely.

Get them moving.

"Bollocks to it all," he said. "I've had enough of this buggering about in here. This is obviously a job for the boffins, and I'm guessing the brass will send the real specialists to relieve us. So let's go back upstairs to the wee hut, shut the door on this thing, and drink tea until they get here."

"No argument from me, Cap," Wiggins said. "I just about pished myself in there."

"To be fair," Hynd said, "you don't usually need an excuse."

The humor wasn't quite as natural as usual, but Banks appreciated the sarge trying, and the men all laughed, albeit without much joy in it.

But it's a start. Now, get them out of here.

He saw sweat glisten on some of the men's faces, not from fear, but from the temperature in the hangar, which appeared to have stabilized somewhere in the 60s Fahrenheit, positively balmy compared to the Antarctic air just beyond the dome.

Hell, they shouldn't have bothered with the saucer. They could have conquered the world without a fight if they'd given us the secret of this kind of heating.

The hut out on the ice was going to feel frigid after this, but he couldn't bear the thought of spending any more time this close to the empty saucer. His experience among the stars had left him wrung out and shaken, and all he wanted to do was to breathe fresh air again and feel real salt water spray on his cheeks.

"Cally, you and Hughes on point. Wilkes and Patel next up, Wiggins is with me, Sarge and Parker, watch our back. Double time, let's get the flock out of here. Silent running until we're topside."

*

Cally pushed the hangar door open and checked the corridor before turning and giving a thumb and forefinger okay. The squad moved out. As soon as the double door closed at their back, the temperature dropped, although the golden glow stayed with them for the first ten yards of the tunnel. It was only when they left the limits of its light and had to revert to their night-vision goggles that Banks felt some of the tension flow out of him, tension he hadn't realized he'd been holding onto since waking on the floor of the hangar. Each step took him farther from the dance in the dark, and he felt some of his sense of purpose return at the same time as the beat of the rhythm slowly faded from his muscle memory.

He wasn't given time to enjoy it. Before they even got halfway down the corridor, the double door at the far end opened. A blast of colder air hit them, then tall shadowed figures stepped into the doorway and walked forward, calmly and steadily.

"What the fuck is this now?" Wiggins whispered at Banks' side.

Banks didn't want to speculate – didn't dare to, for he was afraid that he knew the answer. He saw their eyes first, milky white, almost silver in the night vision. There were at least a dozen of them, led by a tall man in the unmistakable dark uniform and peaked hat. Even in the dim light, the black-on-white swastika was clearly visible on his arm.

It was the oberst. The commander of the base was leading his team. Banks had finally found the corpses he'd been searching for. Or rather, they had found him.

The cold dead filled the tunnel ahead.

*

"What the fuck is this now?" Wiggins repeated loudly.

"It's fucking trouble, that's what it is," Hynd replied.

"Ears in, lads," Banks said, and slid the plastic plugs in before checking his magazine. He had a full load in the mag and spare clips in his vest, but even as the dead walked, still calm and measured, up the corridor toward them, he knew he wasn't ready to fire on unarmed men, not when he still wasn't sure of the situation.

"They were fucking dead, Sarge," Wiggins said. "You saw them. We all saw them. Fucking devious Nazi wankers."

Wiggins looked ready to start shooting, and Banks stopped him simply by putting a hand on the man's shoulder.

"Not now, eh, lad? Not yet anyway. Keep a lid on it."

Wiggins had the sense to go quiet, but his eyes betrayed what Banks guessed they were all feeling.

This just isn't possible.

But he couldn't, no matter how hard he tried, make himself believe in dead men walking – it went against everything he'd seen in his years of service. Once you're down, there's no coming back; he'd seen it often enough to know the truth of it. So he wasn't about to order a shooting gallery.

But when he turned to look back toward the hangar bay and saw the golden glow showing through the windows, he knew he also wasn't ready to retreat, not to a place where he'd so recently been so vulnerable.

"Stand ready," he said quietly. "We don't know what we're dealing with yet. But we do know they are, as Wiggins here put it, fucking devious Nazi wankers, so don't let them get too close. And watch my back."

Banks stepped forward before he could have second thoughts. He had his rifle in hand, pointed straight at the approaching German officer, ready to shoot at the slightest provocation. The man – the impossibly dead man – kept coming, as did the men behind him, a mixture roughly half split of military and civilians, all with the same milk-white eyes glowing silver in the night vision. Banks' finger closed on the trigger, ready to shoot, but the tall officer slowed five yards away from him and came to a stop. The other Germans stopped behind him, and the tunnel fell quiet.

Banks felt the cold coming off the bodies of the dead, as if they weren't composed of flesh at all, but somehow manufactured, perfect mannequins carved from ice. The pale eyes of the oberstleutnant started straight at Banks, unblinking. His lips were gray-blue where they should be red, his skin smooth, almost translucent, like alabaster. Veins, as blue as his lips, showed proud just beneath the surface. Banks was too far away to see any pulse, but he wouldn't have been surprised if there wasn't one.

"What happened here?" Banks asked, aware as he spoke that he was attempting a conversation with a man he'd seen most definitely dead not too many hours before. The German did not reply, but his head cocked slightly to one side, as if listening.

"What happened to you?" Banks continued. "We're here to help."

The officer raised his left hand and pointed, over Bank's shoulder, toward the hangar. The gaze of the white eyes stayed fixed on Banks the whole time, but the intent was clear enough.

"You want to go through there? No, I don't think that's a good idea," Banks said.

The officer kept staring and pointing. The ranks of dead men behind him inched forward, each of them, in parade ground step, taking a short pace up the tunnel.

"Stop right there. That's far enough," Banks said, and showed the German the rifle. If it gave the frozen oberstleutnant any pause, it didn't show. The officer's pale blue lips moved, as if uttering a command, and he pointed again with his left arm. Although no sound came, the order had been given.

This time when the dead men took a step, it was a full one.

*

"Cap?" Hynd said behind Banks.

Banks heard the tension in the sergeant's voice. He took two steps back. The German officer took two steps forward, followed immediately by the dead behind him, who again moved as one in military precision. They stopped, and the oberstleutnant stared at Banks, and pointed up the tunnel toward the hangar with his left hand.

"Cap?" Hynd said again in a whisper. "Maybe we should just let them pass. Let them go wherever the fuck it is they want to go."

"Give them access to that saucer? No fucking way. They might look like dead men, but these are fucking Nazis, man. I'm not letting them near anything that might be a weapon."

"So what then?" the sergeant asked.

The matter was taken out of Banks' hands when the oberstleutnant pointed again, and began to walk forward, faster now, the dead stepping in time behind him.

"Fuck this for a game of soldiers," Wiggins shouted, and for once, Banks agreed with him.

"Fire," he shouted.

*

The tunnel filled with the crack and roar of rifle fire. If the Germans had been flesh, the assault would have reduced them to bloody scraps of red meat, but Banks was dismayed to see that none of them fell under the shots. The squad was hitting their targets. Bits of ice flew where the shots clipped shoulder or skull, but in the main, the bullets seemed to have no effect at all. Banks took careful aim and hit the oberstleutnant in the chest, saw a small hole in the uniform at the impact site, but the tall pale-eyed figure didn't so much as flinch, just kept coming forward at the same steady pace.

They kept firing.

Cally had to step back to reload. Hughes stepped up in his place, just ahead of Banks, and was the closest of the squad members as the approaching German officer took three more steps forward. Banks saw that the private had moved too far ahead of the rest of the squad and was isolated a few paces in front of the others.

"Hughes, fall back, lad," Banks shouted, but it was too late. The German officer was almost within arms' length of the private, who fired three rounds, point blank, into the dead man's face. One hit the milky white left eye and blew it into icy shards, but the oberst kept coming, ignoring the weapon and reaching out for the man. Pale hands caught Hughes by the neck, and the man's eyes rolled up as he fell to one side. Banks stepped in and slammed the butt of his weapon against the dead man's head, chipping off more spattering flakes of ice and frozen flesh. The oberst's grip tightened on Hughes' throat, and Banks heard the sound of the private's neck breaking even above the roar of the gunfire.

There was no time for mourning. The dead man dropped Hughes, already forgotten, and took another pace up the corridor. Banks stepped up quickly, put the barrel of his weapon in the German's left ear and fired, three rounds that should have blown the head apart. The reaction wasn't as conclusive as Banks had hoped, and he only managed to blow a fist-sized hole where the ear had been, sending red-tainted shards of ice flying, but it was enough to drop the officer to the ground. Banks kicked the dead man's head for good measure and immediately regretted it – it felt like kicking a solid piece of ice-cold stone.

He kept an eye on the other dead Germans, but none moved to attack him as he bent and with his left hand grabbed Hughes' collar and dragged the dead weight back toward the rest of the squad.

He saw that Wilkes was struggling with another of the dead Germans, with Patel trying desperately to wrench a cold blue hand from Wilkes' left arm. Sergeant Hynd had obviously seen how Banks dealt with the German officer. The sergeant stepped up and put three rounds into the German's ear. The body fell to the floor like a sack of cold rocks.

The ranks of the dead took another step toward them, stepping up to stand just behind where the dead Oberst lay on the ground.

"Fall back," Banks shouted again, and this time, the squad was all able to comply. Cally and Parker took charge of Hughes and dragged him away while Banks, Wiggins, and Hynd covered Wilkes and Patel. Wilkes looked pale and pained, but was able to walk, and brushed away Patel's helping hand.

"Stop being a bloody auld woman," he said. "I'm fine."

Banks checked the corridor as they backed away toward the hangar.

The cold dead stood still and unmoving behind the two toppled bodies on the ground. The oberst twitched, twice, then, as if doing a press-up, pushed himself up off the floor. The movements were slow and stiff, almost stylized, but ten seconds later, the officer was standing upright at the front of the ranks of the dead.

Banks knew that the oberst had been shot in the left eye – he'd seen the crater for himself. But when the officer looked up and stared along the corridor, it was with two pale, milky eyes, each as round and iced over as the other.

*

The squad backed away fast toward the hangar. When they reached the double door and went through, Wiggins moved to close the doors behind them.

"No, leave it. I want to see those bastards coming," Banks said. "Leave the doors open, but barricade the entrance with tables, chairs, whatever you can find lying around here. It's deep into injury time and we're one-nil down, lads. We make our stand here, or not at all."

"You heard the captain," Hynd shouted. "Arseholes and elbows, get a fucking move on."

Wiggins, Parker, and McCally moved quickly to drag tables over and overturn them in the doorway, stacked such that they blocked the entrance up to almost head height, and were jammed tight between the walls of the tunnel just in front of the doorway, holding the doors open.

McCally put his shoulder against the barricade, testing its strength. It didn't give, and he turned to give Banks an okay sign with thumb and forefinger. Banks stepped forward and looked over. He had a clear view down the length of the corridor. Far down in the shadows, almost at the limit of what he could make out in the dark, the ranks of dead Germans still stood where they had left them, the tall oberstleutnant at their front. As yet, they showed no inclination to come any closer.

Banks called McCally, Wiggins, and Parker over.

"You three are up first. Keep an eye on the buggers, Cally. If they so much as twitch, shout."

"Twitch? They're already fucking dead, Cap," Wiggins replied. "How the fuck are they up and moving?"

Banks knew they all had questions – he had plenty of his own, but he had no answers to give them, and turned away to see to Hughes, fearing the worst. Hynd was bent over the fallen man and turned at Banks' approach. He shook his head and confirmed what Banks already knew.

"He was gone as soon as that fucker broke his neck," the sarge said.

"Poor sod," Banks replied. "No more, do you hear me, Sarge? One down is one too many."

Hynd nodded, and Banks helped him drag Hughes' body over to rest sitting upright against the wall near the door. Banks closed the private's eyes before turning away, relieved in a way to see that there had been a dead stare looking back at him, and not a pair of milky marbles.

"We should maybe watch him," Hynd said, keeping his voice low so that the three at the doorway wouldn't hear him. Patel, who was helping Wilkes out of his jacket and flack vest, heard it clear enough though, and let out a harsh laugh.

"He's hardly going to get up and walk, is he?" he said.

Hynd replied first.

"That's exactly what I'm worried about, lad. You saw those fuckers out in the corridor, and you know they were dead fuckers themselves when we saw them earlier. So, we watch Hughes, and we watch him close, until we're sure."

Patel looked like he might reply, then looked like Banks felt, that there were no words, no questions that made any kind of sense here. All chat stalled as Wilkes finally got stripped off enough that they saw what had happened to his arm. A black handprint, as livid as any tattoo, curled around his biceps. When Banks moved closer, he saw that the skin itself was dead and crisp, as if it had been burned rather than frozen. Wilkes winced as he flexed the arm, all color draining from his face, and livid red cracks appeared in the wound, like volcanic fissures in a lava field.

"Don't do that, lad," Banks said. "You're not helping. Let Patel get you bandaged up. We're going to need you and your gun at the barricade."

"It hurts like a fucking burn, Cap," Wilkes said. "Here's a wee tip for all of you. Don't let one of these buggers near you."

Hynd answered first again.

"Aye, we get that. And you saw how Cap here put the officer down. Don't let them touch you, but get close enough to plug them in the noggin. That seems to be the only way to stop them."

"Stop them? Did we do that, Sarge? Are they stopped?" Patel asked. This time, it was Hynd who didn't have the answers.

Banks left Patel and the sarge to tend to Wilkes' wound. He checked with McCally and got a shake of the head in reply – all was still quiet in the corridor. He reluctantly turned his attention to the thing he'd been trying to avoid ever since they'd returned to the hangar – the impossible saucer at their backs, silently hovering six inches off the floor. It looked like he could step over and push it with a finger to get it moving, but although he didn't know much, he knew that would be a spectacularly bad idea in a day full of plenty of bad ideas already.

He didn't move too close to the saucer. There was too much heat radiating from the glowing golden lines on the floor for one thing, and, for another thing, he felt the tug of the dark places between the stars, felt the call of that strange hypnotic dance that had taken him under its spell. It was seductive, far too much so. He'd lost one man here already, and if he gave in to the needs of the saucer, he was liable to lose even more, if not them all.

The gold of the circles reflected in the almost mirror-like sheen of the saucer's metal, the glow seeming to radiate outward, threatening to spill out of the circles and wash across the hangar. They'd obviously started something by entering the thing in the first place, and Banks wasn't at all sure he wanted to know what ending he was being led to.

Almost reluctantly, he dragged his gaze away. The things in the corridor were his prime concern at the moment, and how to best protect his squad from the menace. He had no idea how the dead had managed to avoid the squad's detention or where they'd been hiding after their disappearance, or how they were even up and walking, given that they were clearly fucking dead.

Too many questions, and no answers.

But they're here now. And that's all I've got to go on.

The relief mission would be here, experts, and sooner rather than later, or so he hoped. His only job now was to keep his squad alive long enough for them to be rescued. But when he turned away from the saucer, it was with a touch of regret. The dance in the dark was still there, still waiting.

And a part of him wanted to dance with it.

- 9 -

Hynd stood by the meters and gauges when Banks walked away from the saucer.

"Do you have the slightest fucking clue what this shite is, Cap? Like, how it works, what the fuck they were trying to do here?"

Banks jerked a thumb back at the saucer.

"They were trying – succeeding if those photographs are to be believed – in flying this thing using power they've got from Churchill's messed-up plan. My guess would be it was to be another V-weapon – which would be fucking ironic if we found any actual rat-munching wee green men. But, somehow, and thankfully, they fucked up and it all went quiet."

"Until we came and fucked it up again?"

"Exactly. Now the best thing we can do is keep our hands off and wait for the boffins. I hope to fuck they know how to deal with it, for I don't have a fucking clue."

"And in the meantime?"

"We hold the line. We stand. What else can we do?"

*

They were given another ten minutes grace, just long enough for Hynd to have a smoke, then Parker called out from the barricade.

"We've got incoming. The bastards are on the move."

Banks didn't have to give an order. As if they'd all been waiting for this moment, the squad moved to take their places, every man with rifle already unslung and ear-plugs being pushed into place.

There was only enough room for four of them to stand abreast behind the makeshift barricade. Parker, Wiggins, McCally, and Hynd lined up first, with Banks holding back alongside Wilkes and Patel, ready to step forward when anyone needed to reload. Banks saw Wilkes wince when he hefted his rifle.

"You going to be okay with that arm, lad?" he asked. Wilkes smiled grimly.

"I've going to have to be, Cap. I owe these fuckers payback for Hughes if nothing else."

Banks was grateful to see there was no questions forthcoming from the squad, no pondering about the reality of what was in front of them. They were trained to face whatever turned up, whether it was Afghan hill guerillas, Mexican drug gangs, or a horde of fucking Nazi ice zombies.

At least this lot won't be shooting back at us.

He expected no less from McCally and Hynd, as they'd both been with him among the high weirdness on the Russian boat off Baffin Island, but he was glad to see that the newer recruits to the team were as calm and controlled as he could wish for.

He looked between Parker and McCally, over the top of the upturned tables. He didn't have his night goggles on, so it was dark down the far end of the tunnel, but not so dark that he couldn't see the approaching figures. Once again, the tall oberst took the front, and even at a distance of twenty yards, his pale eyes stared deep into Banks' soul. The German officer raised his left hand and pointed up the tunnel then led the rest of the dead forward, all of them walking in perfect step at the same slow, measured pace as before. Again, Banks was reminded of a parade ground drill. Then another, more apt, analogy came to him.

They're no more than puppets. But who is the puppeteer? And where is he?

"Go for head shots, lads," Banks said. "And short, concentrated bursts. I only brought that fucker down last time by putting the barrel right up against his head. So wait until they're close enough that you're sure of a target, then hit them hard. We've got your back, so duck out the way if you get in trouble. Plugs in – this is going to get noisy."

Banks pushed his own earplugs all the way in, and just had time to note that they also served to lessen the vibration rising from the saucer. He hadn't really noticed it until there was an absence of it, but suddenly his thought processes felt sharp again, less clouded by the dance of the darkness and stars. He pushed the thought away, something to be considered later, if there was a later.

The dead Germans moved up to within ten yards of the barricaded doorway. Banks had a good long look at the oberstleutnant. His eye, and the chunk of flesh around his ear, had apparently regenerated, and there was no sign of any damage to his uniform, although Banks clearly remembered the black hole in his jacket, the hole he had put there himself. Not only did these fuckers come back from the dead, their clothes came back too, repaired as good as new.

I think we're in trouble.

"Fire at will," he shouted, and the crack of gunfire echoed loudly around the hangar.

*

Banks' squad picked their targets well, each taking the dead man directly in front of them. Banks counted sixteen of the dead, in four ranks of four. The first rank ate up bullets as the four men fired volley after volley, the icy dead still walking forward at the same steady pace.

Five yards now. They'd be at the barricade in seconds. The oberst looked Banks in the eye. His mouth, gray lips little more than a fish-like slit, never moved but Banks had a distinct impression that the bugger was smiling.

"The officer. Put the fucking officer down," he shouted. "You saw how they stopped the last time."

Hynd and Parker both moved their aim at the same time and concentrated on the officer. Banks and Patel stepped forward to aim between them at the men's original targets.

Six rounds hit the oberstleutnant in the face in less than a second, and this time the tall figure teetered, like a tree about to fall. Banks swung his own weapon round and added his effort to the rest.

Four yards now, soon to be within grabbing distance.

Nine rounds hit the German officer in the head, and this time he did fall, going down with a solid thud that sent a vibration through the floor. Banks felt it thrum in the soles of his feet even through his boots.

The other attackers stopped in their tracks, as if their driving force had been unplugged.

We got the fucking puppetmaster.

"Put them down. Put all these fuckers down," Banks shouted.

The corridor became a shooting gallery. Banks was dismayed at how much of their ammo they had to expend just to put one of the things to the ground, and all of the squad had to step back to reload at least once before he was able to call a cease-fire.

Thin smoke hung above them, and his weapon was hot in his hands. Spent shells lay all around and despite the protection of the plugs, his ears rang with slowly fading echoes – he knew it would be many minutes before his hearing would be anything approaching normal.

The sixteen bodies lay in a heap in the corridor, and although Banks stood there for long minutes watching, none of them moved. The tall officer lay, partially pinned, beneath two civilians, and it was him that Banks watched most particularly, ready to fire again at the slightest provocation. But there was no sound, no movement.

Behind him he heard, as if in the distance, Parker and Wiggins loudly congratulating each other on a job done, but Banks wasn't ready yet to join in any celebration. He'd put the

German officer down before, put a hole in the dead man's chest, taken out an eye, and still hadn't slowed him much.

Just because the oberstleutnant had been put down again didn't mean this was over, not by a long way.

*

Once he was sure the dead were really down this time, he let the men break off for a smoke while he and Hynd stood at the barricade, looking back along the corridor. He felt heat come in waves at his back from the saucer, but kept his gaze forward as the sergeant spoke.

"How long until the relief team get here, Cap?"

The man's voice echoed as if coming up from out of a deep well, but Banks understood him well enough.

"Too fucking long," he replied. He only half paid attention – he was considering going over the barricade and pounding the oberstleutnant's head with his rifle butt until there was nothing left but slush. The trouble was, he still wasn't sure that would be enough to keep the dead man down. Somehow, this was all due to that fucking saucer.

I turned it on. Now I wish I knew how to turn the bloody thing off.

He forced his attention back to the sarge.

"We have to stand," he said. "I can't think what else we can do – unless you've got any bright ideas?"

"I suppose flying yon thing out of here isn't an option?" Hynd said, jerking his thumb at the saucer.

"Don't even think of it," Banks replied, thinking again of the dark and the seductive dance in the stars. "I'm getting no closer to that fucker than I need to. None of us should."

Hynd was about to reply when they heard a metallic clang, far off, away down the corridor and coming from the living quarters beyond.

"I counted sixteen here," Hynd said quietly.

"Aye, me too. We both know there were more than that the

first time we came in. And we don't ken how many more in total."

Hynd echoed Bank's earlier thought back at him.

"This isn't over, is it, Cap?"

Banks didn't answer. He didn't have to.

Another clang echoed through the base.

*

He stayed at the barricade for ten more minutes, watching the corridor. None of the bodies on the ground moved, and it didn't look like they were going to. They melted, having encroached into the zone of heat being washed through the hangar by the gold circles on the floor. A trickle of dirty fluid ran away down the corridor toward the living quarters from underneath the pile of dead. Within the space of only two or three minutes, the bodies were little more than rounded boulders of ice, nothing left of the men they had been. Even more disconcerting, if that were possible, every part of them melted down, bone and hair, skin and muscle – including their clothing, everything impossibly turned to dirty water. A stream ran, snaking, away down the corridor into the darkness, as if fleeing from the heat and light coming from the hangar.

Hynd arrived at Banks' side and looked over the barricade. He stood there watching the melting bodies, silent, for a long time before turning around.

"Maybe we shouldn't tell the lads about this, Cap," he said quietly. "They're all good men and are keeping it together, but this shite is nae doin' their nerves much good."

"Mine neither," Banks replied. "But at least these icy fuckers have buggered off for now."

"But for how long?"

That was another question for which Banks didn't have an answer.

Another thought struck him, and he turned quickly to where they'd left Hughes' body against the wall. He didn't know whether to be relieved or not to see that the corpse was still sitting in the same position where they'd left him and hadn't melted away like the others.

But that's not to say it still might happen.

"See if you can find something to wrap Hughes in," he said to Hynd. "We'll be taking him with us when we go."

"We're going?"

It wasn't until the sergeant asked that Banks realized he had made his mind up some time ago.

"I think that's the best idea," he replied. "Yon saucer creeps me out about as much as those fucking ice zombies. I'd rather take our chances outside in the hut."

"I think the lads will agree with you there, Cap," Hynd said, and left Banks to go to talk to the men.

Banks turned back to the barricade, pulled on his night vision, and tried to see into the darkness at the far end of the tunnel, but all he saw was the stream of dirty water running away into the black.

- 10 -

The squad knocked up a makeshift stretcher from the top of one of the tables that made up the barricade, then McCally and Hynd dragged the remaining tables aside to clear the doorway. The wood screeched loudly on the floor as they moved it, the noise echoing away down the corridor. Banks called for quiet, and they stood, listening, but there was no response, although Banks remembered only too well the metallic clangs they'd heard earlier. He didn't expect this to go easily.

"We do this fast, or we don't do it at all," Banks said. "Down the corridor, then up the stairwell, out the door and down to the hut. Anything gets in our way, we take it out hard. Are we all clear on that?"

Wiggins, Parker, Patel, and Wilkes each had a corner of the table with Hughes' body on it. Before getting ready to move out, all of the men had taken a look at what was now only a smear of slushy water on the corridor floor, but no one had spoken of it, and Banks wasn't about to be the first to broach the subject.

He let McCally and Hynd take point, and he held back, letting the four stretcher-bearers pass him so that he could bring up the rear. He took a final look at the saucer as he left. It still did nothing but sit and hover, vibrating slightly just off the floor, but he felt its call, heard the stars sing in the blackness inside it, and yet again he had to fight the impulse to give himself over to its pleasures. It took all of his strength to turn his back on the golden glow and follow the squad down the corridor.

*

The first thing Banks noticed was how far the heat and light now penetrated. He didn't have to do up his jacket or pull down the night-vision goggles until they were halfway along the tunnel corridor.

Despite the clearer vision, they were making slower progress than he'd hoped, for the floor felt slippery underfoot now where the water had run and frozen again. They'd have gone faster without having to bring Hughes' body with them, but they didn't leave men behind.

And especially not when there's a chance of them getting up and walking around.

Wiggins almost lost his footing, and Banks had to move up next to the makeshift stretcher to steady it. Hughes' eyes had opened again, and the dead man stared at him, accusing.

I'll get you home, lad. It's all I can do for you now.

Hynd and McCally reached the double door at the end of the corridor first, but didn't open it until the whole squad had come together. Banks squeezed passed the stretcher-bearers to join the other two at the doors.

"Remember, we do this fast," Banks said in a low voice. "Through, up the stairs and away to the hut, slicker than shite off a shovel. We stop for nothing."

He opened the double door.

They wouldn't be going anywhere in a hurry. Ranks of the frozen dead stood immediately outside the doorway, completely blocking their path to the main stairwell upward. At the lead of them stood the tall oberst, once again clad in full uniform, peaked hat firmly on his head, the jacket immaculate and free from any bullet holes, the Swastika showing sharp and clear on his armband. The German looked up as the door opened, stared straight at Banks with two milk-white eyes, raised his left hand, and pointed over Banks' shoulder, back along the corridor toward the hangar. At the same time, he took a step forward. The ranks of the dead, four wide and at least eight rows of them that Banks could see, came forward in step, like clockwork dolls that had just been set in motion.

*

"How many times do we need to put this fucker down?" Wiggins said at Banks' back.

"Third time's the charm," Banks said, but didn't give the order to fire. He'd seen how much ammo they'd needed at the last attack; they didn't have the firepower to force their way past the ranks ahead. He had a longing look at the stairwell, their path to freedom, but there were too many of the dead between the doorway and the stairs. They might make it, they might not, but he'd probably lose men in the process. Having come this far, he was loath to give up their position, but he knew he had little choice; Hughes dead eyes still accused him; he wasn't ready to lose another squad member.

"Back up," he said as the Germans came forward at the same slow pace as previously. "Back to the hangar. If we can't shoot them all, at least the heat will get them."

They backed away, once again slowed by the stretcher-bearers and being wary of the ice on the floor. The dead came through the doorway four abreast after them.

Banks, McCally, and Hynd put themselves between the attack and the men carrying Hughes' body, and for a while they managed to maintain an even distance to the tall German officer as they went back up the corridor, but calamity struck near the halfway point.

Somebody slipped. Banks didn't see who it was, he only heard the clatter and thud, then an echoing crack as the bed of the table on which Hughes' body was lying split. In the time it took Wilkes and Patel to heft the dead body between then and get moving again, the oberst had stepped up almost face to face with the rearmost men of the squad.

Banks stared into the dead-white eyes, and felt the icy cold wash off the officer as the German raised his left hand again and pointed up the corridor toward the hangar.

"The answer is still no," Banks said. "So why don't you fuck off back to wherever you came from."

The oberst took another step forward.

Banks put three quick rounds into its face, then turned away.

"Leg it," he shouted. "Back to the door, and fast. Let's see if we can hold them off long enough for the heat to stop them."

*

They slipped and slid their way at a flat run all the way back up the corridor, arriving at the hangar doorway just in time for Wilkes and Patel to dump Hughes body unceremoniously by the side. Then it was a frantic few seconds while they arranged a new barricade, although this one was nowhere near as sturdy as their earlier attempt and was only waist rather than neck high. By the time they got it in place, the approaching dead were less than ten paces away.

"At least it's fucking warmer up here," Wiggins said. That was an understatement; the temperature in the hangar appeared to have risen even more during their short absence, forcing the squad to unzip their outer jackets. Parker started to shuck his off.

"No," Banks said loudly. "Stay ready for cold-weather action. We don't know when this is all going to go sideways on us."

Wiggins laughed at that.

"We're pretty much as far off to left-field as we can get, don't you think, Cap?"

"I wouldn't bet my house on that, lad," Hynd replied.

"I wouldn't bet your house on it either, Sarge," McCally said, then there was no time for talk.

The dead kept coming forward, but now Banks saw that they were already melting, with icy slush, like semi-solid sweat, leaching off their bodies and clothes as they approached the hangar doorway.

"We only need to hold until the heat gets them," he said. "Remember, short controlled bursts, head shots only. Take that officer down first, all of us at once. On my signal."

McCally, Wiggins, Patel, and Wilkes knelt on the ground and aimed over the top of the edge of the barricade while Banks joined Hynd and Parker in standing just behind them.

The oberstleutnant was still in the front rank of the oncoming dead. Banks saw that his most recent shots had taken out the left eye and blown off part of the cheek below it, but once again, he hadn't done any damage of any substance. The tall officer raised his left arm to point again.

"Enough of this fucking shite," Wiggins said, and Banks tended to agree.

"Fire," he shouted.

*

The concentrated volley at close range blew the oberstleutnant's face and most of the front of his head away, spraying ice fragments all through the tunnel. The body swayed, its left arm still pointing into the hangar, then finally toppled. When it hit the ground, the German officer shattered into fragments, slushy ice skittering across the floor.

"We got the fucker," Wiggins shouted in triumph, but this time the ranks of the dead did not stop when the leader fell. They kept coming forward at the same steady pace.

Whatever is in charge of all of this bollocks is learning.

"Fire at will!" Banks shouted.

The squad didn't need any other urging. Fragments of ice flew, shots cracked in a seemingly endless roar and every few seconds another of the frozen men toppled to smash on the floor as little more than rapidly melting, slushy ice. The heat was taking its toll on the attack almost as much as their weaponry. But still they kept coming, their sheer weight of numbers forcing them inch by slow inch closer to the barricade.

Wilkes and Parker both had to reload at the same time. The momentary weakness in the field of fire gave the iced dead an opportunity to shuffle six more inches onward, although three more of their number crashed to fragments almost at the same time. The floor of the corridor immediately ahead of the barricade was now awash with icy slush and dirty water. Thin smoke hung just below the roof of the tunnel, almost obscuring the ceiling completely and making it appear that the frozen dead were lurching forward through an autumnal fog, a scene straight out of a gothic horror.

"Hold them back," Banks shouted, and shot another full in a face that looked more like melted wax than flesh. All of the front rank of the attack were melting faster now, and the waves of heat from the circles around the saucer made Bank's back feel like it was being slowly toasted under a hot grill. The squad used up ammo at a prodigious rate, but they were only just managing to hold off the onslaught, and a quick mental calculation made Bank's heart sink.

We're not going to make it.

*

The nearest rank of the dead stepped up to within two feet of the barricade. The squad was now in as much danger from ricochet as from anything else. Hynd had to step back to reload, and Banks knew that his own mag was near empty, and that some of the others must also be getting close to having to switch magazines. There was no way they'd be given either the time or the space to do it.

He only had one option left to him. He didn't like it, but it was the only way to avoid losing more of the men.

"Back up," he called. "Everybody into the gold circles."

"Fuck that. There's nothing to stop them coming right after us, Cap," Wiggins said.

"I said, back up. Let them come. They won't be able to take the heat."

The men moved as one unit, still shooting as they walked backward toward the glowing gold lines. The barricade quickly became little more than cracked wood and splinters as the dead came through. The front rank fell almost immediately as the heat took them down to slush in seconds, but the second rank got farther into the hangar, and the third rank farther still.

Banks' team was now backed up as far as they could go without stepping into the glowing circles around the saucer. The heat here was almost baking, threatening to set their clothing smoldering.

"Quickly. All the way," Banks shouted. "Into the circles then cease fire."

He let the others pass him, then stepped over the two concentric gold lines. As soon as he stepped fully into the inner circle, the heat fell away. He saw that the warmth still radiated out in the hangar, and his hunch had been right – it was proving too much for the approaching attack. Another rank of the icy dead fell to the floor, this time fully liquid when they hit the floor with a splash of nothing more than dirty water.

The squad stopped firing and the hangar fell silent save for an audible hum from the saucer. The remaining ranks of the dead stopped in the doorway by the ruined remnants of the barricade, as if an order had been issued to come no farther.

Something's coming.

He didn't know how he knew, but he felt it, the same old gut instinct that had always served him well. He saw that Hynd had sensed it too, an old soldier's hunch that the worst was still to come that had them both keep their weapons raised and pointed at the doorway.

But the attack, when it came, came from elsewhere.

*

Banks tasted the impossibility again, the tang of salt water, cold at his lips. A sibilant sound echoed and joining the humming from the saucer—distant chanting, getting louder. To a man, the ranks of the dead in the doorway lifted their left arms and pointed, straight at the saucer. They didn't step forward, but moved aside to let someone—something—through. The tall German officer, once more in pristine full uniform, walked to the front of the rank. He too raised his left arm and pointed, and once again, Banks thought he sensed rather than saw a smile on his face.

The saucer hummed louder, the golden glow intensified, and Banks immediately realized his mistake, possibly a fatal one. The icy dead did not want to get to the saucer. They'd got what they'd wanted all along.

They've got us right where they want us.

Banks and the squad were all inside the golden circle as the chanting rose louder and louder, but not loud enough that Banks didn't hear the crack as the saucer door opened at his back, even despite his earplugs.

- 11 -

"Cap?" Hynd said. "What the fuck is this now?"

Banks looked back to the doorway. The German officer stepped backward, and was soon lost in the shadows, off and away escaping from the heat that meant the ranks of dead in the doorway were melting fast.

We should make a run for it. We might not get another chance.

But the order stayed unspoken as the chanting rose louder still, ringing loudly in his ears, washing all thoughts from his mind except for the call of the dance in the black. The saucer vibrated like a tuning fork in sympathy. The floor swayed lazily in time. A shout came from somewhere, Hynd by the sound of it, but he was so very far away, and Banks couldn't drag his gaze from the saucer. It rose, almost imperceptibly, lazily, until it now hovered eight inches off the floor.

The chanting again took on the beat that set his whole body shaking, vibrating with the rhythm. His head swam, and it seemed as if the walls of the hangar melted and ran. The light from the high dome above receded into a great distance until it was little more than a pinpoint in a blanket of darkness, and he was alone, in a cathedral of emptiness where nothing existed save the dark and the pounding chant.

He danced.

As he had before, he saw stars, in vast swathes of gold and blue and silver, all dancing in great purple and red clouds that spun webs of grandeur across unending vistas. Shapes moved in and among the nebulae; dark, wispy shadows casting a pallor over whole galaxies at a time, shadows that capered and whirled as the dance grew ever more frenetic, and he knew what they were – his squad, as lost in the great beyond as he was himself. Lost in the dance.

Banks was buffeted, as if by a strong, surging tide, but as the beat grew ever stronger, he cared little. He gave himself to it, lost in the dance, lost in the stars. He didn't know how long he wandered in the space between. He forgot himself, forgot the squad, dancing in the vastness where only rhythm mattered.

He might have been lost forever had not one word, one name, come to mind, a last-ditch defense by his mind to save what was left of his sanity.

Carnacki.

And with that, the memory came full, of the man's journal, and of Carnacki standing, lost, in a place even darker than the hangar, a place as dark as this vastness between the stars. The Englishman's words formed, unbidden at Banks' lips, and he shouted them into the void.

Dhumna Ort!

*

The result was immediate. The chanting stopped as if a switch had been thrown and Banks' vision cleared, slowly, struggling to focus. He looked around; the squad was in the same boat, slowly coming out of whatever fugue had taken them. But the saucer, although still hovering, still glowing, was no longer giving off the audible hum. More importantly than that, there was no sign of any of the frozen dead in the doorway.

Banks calculated the risks, decided they were manageable, and gave the order.

"Time to go, lads," he said. "Move out. Double time."

He was pleased to see that they all responded. When Wilkes and Patel moved to lift Hughes' body, he stopped them.

"No, leave him. We'll be back for him when we can, but we need to move fast, get topside and as far away from this weird shite as we can, and we need to do it right fucking now."

Wilkes looked like he might refuse to leave his friend, but moved when Patel put a hand on his shoulder. McCally and Parker took point and again Banks chose to bring up the rear as they headed out through the doorway.

Third time's a charm.

He lifted a hand to pull down the night-vision goggles, then realized he didn't need them – the main base lights that had been dark since their arrival were now blazing bright. And the farther down the corridor they got, the more they noticed that it wasn't getting any colder – the heating had also kicked in all along the tunnel. Not for the first time, Banks got the impression of being watched, scrutinized by something that had now completely woken up and was most definitely curious.

They met no resistance, and weren't impeded at all by ice. The floor was no longer frozen. Everything, dead flesh and clothing and all had melted away, leaving the squad to splash through dirty water the whole length of the corridor.

McCally and Wiggins stopped at the double door at the far end, and again Banks made his way to the front.

"If those wankers are there, we go through them this time. I've had enough buggering about."

He saw by the squad's faces that they were in agreement. He counted to three with his fingers, then pushed open the doors.

*

The large circular chamber that marked the interior of the main living area was empty – there weren't even any puddles on the floor here. The only other difference from their last visit was that the lights and the heating were on here too now, and the walls ran damp with melting frost. Banks wondered if he went over and looked he might see the German officer sitting at his chair again, now slowly melting down to a puddle, but he wasn't stupid enough to go and try.

The way appeared to be clear.

And this might be the only chance we get.

"Stairs, now," he said, and the squad moved in reply. They made their way quickly up the stairwell and reached the exterior door with no resistance – thankfully there was no body lying on the upper landing, just more dampness and melted frost running down the walls.

He stopped the squad at the exit at the top.

"Cally, with me."

The corporal came to his side, and the two of them pushed open the door. Banks winced at the resulting squeal of metal on metal as the old hinges complained, but if anyone—or anything—apart from them heard, they didn't respond. They looked out over the pathway down to the quay and the quiet bay beyond. There was no sign of any immediate threat.

Banks let the squad exit and then stepped up and out, taking a welcome breath of cold, fresh, air. He was surprised to see that the sky was darkening – they'd been on site for the whole day already.

"Close it," he said, and McCally and Parker moved to comply. The screech of the wheel turning echoed across the still twilight in the bay, but with the closing of the door it felt like a weight had been lifted. What with that, and the fresh air, Banks suddenly felt better, and for the first time in hours, he did not feel the call to the dance of the cosmos. He tugged out his earplugs, and listened, ready to replace them should he hear any hum, feel any compulsion. But all he heard was the soft whistle of a breeze blowing around the huts.

Even looking up toward the ice shelf and seeing the glowing dome of the hangar roof show bright in the growing gloom didn't quell the newly found relief and feeling of freedom.

The men seemed to share his relief, and although they were still at combat readiness, some of the tension of the fight and flight was even now leeching out of them. When they saw him remove his plugs, they followed suit.

"What now, Cap?" Hynd said.

"To the dinghy," he said. "I need to call this shite in. We were ordered to hold in place unless circumstances changed dramatically. Well, I'd say this fucking qualifies. I'm all for getting back to the big boat and waiting there for our relief, and if I get a bollocking for that, then so be it – I'll send the colonel down to yon bloody saucer and see how much he likes it."

That was the most he'd said at any one time all day, but it had brought a broad grin to Hynd's face.

"We're all with you on that, Cap. A wee heat and a drink will suit me just fine."

*

Banks should have known that it wasn't going to be that simple. When he led the squad down the path to the jetty, they found the dingy lying almost totally underwater, sunk where they'd tied it up, a long jagged gash torn along the length of its rubber.

Somebody doesn't want us leaving.

"The radio?" Wiggins asked.

Banks just pointed down into the dark water in reply. He looked out over the bay. It was getting dark fast now, at least as dark as it ever got here, but even so there were no lights showing out on the water. The captain of the icebreaker was as good as his word and had kept out of sight offshore. There was no way to contact him.

Yet again Banks' options had narrowed to a single point of action.

"Looks like we're bedding down in that hut again, lads. I hope nobody minds getting cozy."

"As long as the sarge keeps his hands to himself, we'll be fine," Parker said.

"That's what his wife says too," Wiggins added, and got a cuff on the ear for his cheek. But at least the squad's spirits had lifted, if only a fraction.

It was a start.

*

The shed was indeed cozy, and colder than Banks remembered, although he knew that was a reaction to having spent time in the overheated saucer hangar. It warmed up fast when McCally got the stove fired up.

"Have we got enough fuel to keep that thing going, Cally?" Banks asked.

"Aye, Cap. There's a supply of cut wood in a box underneath it. Enough for a night anyway. We've got plenty of tea and powdered soup too, but there's nothing in the way of solids apart from what we've got in the packs."

"Hard biscuits and soup it is then," Banks replied. "But hopefully our relief will be here before we have to start eating Wiggins."

Wiggins wobbled his stomach with his hands.

"Too much fat anyway, although there's plenty to grab on to, or so the sarge's wife says."

McCally and Parker rustled up soup, and after that brewed up tea for the squad. Banks let them get smokes lit, then brought them all up to speed with everything he'd learned in Carnacki's journal, and his conclusions as to what had happened in the saucer hangar.

"It wants us, needs us I think, to fly that bloody saucer out of here. It wanted us in the hangar all along, and we were daft enough to play right into its hands. We got herded, like fucking sheep."

"Dinnae talk shite, Cap," Wiggins said. "A fucking demon? And Winston fucking Churchill gave it to the Huns? I don't believe in fucking demons. I'm a fucking Protestant. This is black ops propaganda bollocks for sure."

Banks saw that most of the rest of them were just as skeptical, and might have voiced it, if Hynd hadn't spoken up first.

"Yon German officer went down twice and got back up again, out of nowhere too. We all saw it; the fucker melted away to slush one minute then was back in uniform sharp as a pin minutes later. I don't ken much about science, but I ken enough to understand the fucking impossible when I see it. I think Cap's thinking right on this one. You all know me, I'm not a man for all that Holy Joe religious crap. And I was raised a Protestant too and never had any time for saints or angels or demons. But what we've got here might just make me change my mind, at least about the last of those."

The squad fell quiet, even Wiggins subdued by the truth they heard, and saw in the sarge's eyes. Eventually, Wilkes spoke. Banks noticed the private was favoring his injured arm, and the pain showed in the younger man's face, but his voice was steady enough.

"Whatever the fucker is, it killed Hughes. It's going to pay for that. That bastard, demon or not, is going down. And once I'm finished with it, it'll be staying down."

"I'm up for some of that action," Patel said, and the two of them bumped fists.

"Aye, we're all up for some of that," Wiggins said. "But how the fuck do we put it down if it keeps coming back?"

"Maybe we'll just warm things up around here," McCally said, and Wiggins laughed.

"Fuck that for a lark," he replied. "We've all seen that movie. Unless you've got a bottle of whisky somewhere, that's not an ending I'm in a rush to get to. Does anybody here have a single fucking clue how to deal with a demon? Anybody got some Holy Water shoved up their jacksie?"

"It could have killed us all easily," Hynd said quietly. "The fact that it hasn't tells me it wants us for something."

"Flying a fucking UFO?" Wiggins said. "Why would a bloody demon want us to do that?"

"We don't know. That's why they're sending in the experts," Banks replied, and got a laugh from Wiggins in reply.

"There's experts in this shite? Who the fuck would that be? Bernard fucking Quatermass?"

Not for the first time that day, Banks didn't have an answer.

*

Another card game started up around the table with McCally, Parker, and Wiggins taking a hand. Patel and Wilkes got first dibs on a sleep, and each took a bunk, Patel's snores soon vying to be heard over the bids and counter-bids of the card players. Banks stood near the stove, trying to get some heat back inside him. Hynd stood in front of the stove, warming his hands at the grille.

"Can I ask you a question, Cap?" the sarge said.

"Ask ahead," Banks replied. "But at this point, all of you know everything that I know."

"It's about when we stepped into the circles back in the hangar," Hynd said. "The stars and the chanting and the weird shit. You heard and saw all of that, right? It wisnae just a wee dream I was having?"

Banks nodded.

"If it was a dream, I had the same one. Both then, and the first time too when Wiggins and I were inside on our own."

"But those words you shouted, the two Gaelic words? They broke the spell – trance – whatever the fuck it was? It was them that saved us?"

Banks nodded again.

"I think so. I can't see what else got us out. I got lucky and remembered the words I read in the journal."

"Thank fuck that you did, Cap. But Wiggins is right about one thing. This is some bloody weird shite, even for us."

"Aye. I hear you. But with the dinghy and the radio both fucked, all we can do is stay away from that fucking saucer, sit tight here, and wait for the cavalry."

Hynd did a passable impression of Wiggins.

"Bernard fucking Quatermass?"

Banks managed a smile.

"I'll take bloody Flash Gordon if he knows what the fuck is going on here."

*

The card came continued, the hut got warmer, and a fug of thin blue cigarette smoke hung in the air. Everything was calm, and the squad, if not exactly relaxed, were in that state all fighting men knew well, taking advantage of any lull as well as was possible in the circumstances. Wiggins kept up a flow of chat and crudity that meant the men around the table were distracted from having to think, Patel and Wilkes were getting some well-deserved kip.

But Banks himself couldn't settle, and the cigarette smoke was bringing back too many memories of the days when he had indulged – over-indulged – the habit himself. It would be all too easy to walk over to the table and get one lit. He could even imagine the warm smoke, and the hit he would get after such a long time away, but a cigarette was the last thing he needed right now.

He zipped up his jacket, pulled the hood over his ears, and went quickly outside in search of fresher air.

Full night had fallen on the bay, and Banks stood immediately outside the door for long moments, taking time to appreciate the view of the expanse of sky above and the cold blue bay with the ice seeming to twinkle back at the stars.

At first, he thought all was quiet, but the longer he stood, the more the sound came to him, a quiet hum, like a far-off generator. He knew what it must be without having to go looking for it. The saucer was still powered up, and he saw it in his mind, hovering inside the circles in a golden glow that filled the hangar.

Once more, the dance of the stars called to him, the urge to lose himself in the vast blackness.

"Dhumna Ort!" he muttered, and to his relief the hum, and the urge, both faded.

But they did not disappear completely. Suddenly, the sky overhead had lost its charms, and now seemed to lower over him like a dark drape, one that was getting heavier with every passing second. He went back inside, but the distant hum came in with him, and seemed to ring and reverberate in his skull. He went and stood by the stove. Hynd raised an eyebrow in a question, but Banks ignored him and started warming his hands at the grate.

"Dhumna Ort!" he muttered, and the hum faded into the background again, but still did not dissipate completely. It stayed somewhere near the back of his skull, calling relentlessly.

"Dhumna Ort!" he muttered again.

"You okay, Cap?" Hynd said.

Banks nodded and tried to smile.

"Just wishing there was something a wee bit stronger than tea available. I need a drink. I need a lot of drink."

"You and me both, Cap," the sarge replied. "The relief will be here soon, right?"

Banks nodded again, although this time he wasn't able to smile with it, and when Hynd nodded back, there was no smile in reply. When the sarge stepped back over to the card game, Banks stayed at the stove. The image of the hovering saucer was big in his mind, and the hum kept up its call. He turned his back to the table so that the squad wouldn't see him, and muttered the words, almost continuously, his only talisman against the calling.

"Dhumna Ort! Dhumna Ort!"

It kept the monkish chanting and the beat of the dance at a far enough distance for it to be manageable.

For now.

- 12 -

Everything was quiet for several hours, and Banks started to believe the worst might be over, and that they'd be given enough respite to make it through to the arrival of their relief. But all such hopes were dashed when it was time to change shifts and Parker went over to the bunks to wake Wilkes and Patel.

As soon as Wilkes got up out of the bunk, and as if something had been waiting for just that moment, a voice called out from outside, somewhere distant, but loud. It was Hughes – dead Private Hughes – and he was singing at the top of his voice, bellowing in his immediately recognizable off-key shout, somewhere out in the night.

There was a soldier, a Scottish soldier, who wandered far away, and soldiered far away. There was none bolder, with good broad shoulder, he fought in many a fray and fought and won.

"What the fuck kind of bollocks is it this time?" Wiggins said.

"It's Hughes," Wilkes said. "He's alive."

The private stepped forward, heading for the door. Hynd stood to get in his way.

"Dinnae be daft, lad. You saw him. We all saw him. His neck was broken, and he had been dead for hours when we left him back in the hangar."

Wilkes tried to push Hynd aside.

"Aye, we left him. And that was a mistake, wasn't it? The poor bugger has woken up all on his lonesome."

Hynd spoke.

"That's not how it happened, lad. And you bloody know it."

Wilkes shook his head.

"You're right. I thought he was dead. But maybe he's back. Like that Jerry officer."

The singing continued outside.

Because these green hills are not Highland hills, or the island hills there not my lands hills. And as fair as these foreign hills may be, they are not the hills of home.

Hynd put a hand on Wilkes' chest to stop him.

"If he's anything like that Jerry officer, then you don't want anything to do with him. Use your head, lad. Your pal's long gone. You know that."

It was Patel, not Wilkes who replied. He had moved to the door when everyone's attention was on Hynd and Wilkes.

"Aye. But he's our pal. I owe it to him to make sure he's okay. Would you leave one of yours out there on his own?"

He didn't wait for an answer. He opened the door and walked out into the night before anyone had time to move to stop him.

*

The squad only moved once Patel had gone outside. Banks reached the open door first. He hadn't even been aware of doing it, but he had his weapon unslung from his shoulder and was aiming straight ahead, anticipating any attack. He called out.

"Patel, get your arse back in here right now. That's an order."

There was no reply, no sound at all now from outside. Hughes – if it had been him – had stopped singing, and there was only a soft whistle of wind. He felt its cold bite on his cheeks as he reached the doorway. He only got two steps outside, then stopped, although he didn't lower his weapon. The reason Patel had not complied with his order was immediately obvious.

The tall oberst, back in his pristine black uniform, peaked cap, and both pale eyes staring, stood on the path that led to the jetty, with serried ranks four wide of the dead behind him. They all faced the doorway of the hut and the officer had Patel in a half-nelson grip. Banks knew that a simple, sudden movement would be enough to break the man's neck. He looked for Hughes among the frozen ranks, but didn't see the dead man. He heard him again though, the song coming clear across the cold slope from higher up, from the direction of the hangar.

And now this soldier, this Scottish soldier, who wandered far away and soldiered far away, sees leaves are falling, and death is calling. And he will fade away in that far land.

Banks had always previously thought of that particular song as being almost jolly, a tune to bind Scots together during New Year's Eve festivities back home. But hearing it sung by a dead man, as a dirge at almost half speed, it sounded as mournful as any bagpipe lament and it had the same effect, tugging directly at his heart. He had a tear in his eye that he had to brush away to pay full attention to the scene in front of him.

The German officer was still looking straight at Banks. He lifted his free left arm and pointed up at the hangar, at the same time tightening his grip on Patel's neck. Patel's throat was too constricted for him to speak, and Banks saw the pleading in his eyes clear enough. And the oberstleutnant's meaning was clearer yet.

Get back to the hangar. Go into the saucer, or I will kill this man.

Banks was of a mind to comply – he'd lost men in the call of duty before, but always when he knew what he was fighting for. This current situation had him so conflicted he scarcely knew what to do for the best, but he knew he couldn't just let Patel be a pawn in the bigger battle. He was about to nod to give his assent, but Private Wilkes had other ideas.

"Let him go, you wanker," the private shouted and barreled out of the door, knocking Banks aside in the process. The oberst hardly moved, but as Wilkes ran forward and aimed the butt of his rifle at the frozen head, the officer made two movements almost simultaneously. The first was with his right arm, and the crack of Patel's neck breaking echoed around the still night air of the bay. The second, with his left arm held out stiff, hit Wilkes in the chest like a sledgehammer. The private's ribs caved in under the blow, then Wilkes was off his feet and hurtling away, limbs sprawled, to smash, just a bundle of bloody wet flesh now, against the wall of a neighboring hut. Banks had two men downed in as many seconds.

Hynd and McCally stepped out, weapons raised to flank Banks.

"Cap?" Hynd said, and Banks knew it was a request to start shooting. But that hadn't worked out well for them so far.

The oberst raised his left arm again and pointed up toward the hangar. Banks considered it, but now it felt like it would be an insult to the two dead men to give in to the demand. He raised his voice and spoke so that his squad behind him would hear the conviction in his voice. They needed to hear it, and Banks needed to say it.

"The answer's still fucking no," he said, then turned to Hynd.

"Back inside, right now. We don't have the firepower to take them down. We need to try something else."

The others complied with his order and seconds later, the five of them were back in the hut. McCally closed the door, but within seconds, something pounded heavily on the other side, the force of it shaking the door in its frame. At the same time, a layer of frost grew, impossibly fast, across the inside surface. McCally had to forcibly peel his gloved hand from the door; it had been flash-frozen against the wood in seconds. Banks saw his breath condense in the air and felt cold bite at his nose and lips.

"Heat. We need more heat," he shouted. "Get that fucking stove stoked as high as you can get it, Cally."

The corporal moved quickly to the stove and threw cut logs into the open grate, as many as the small stove could hold comfortably. All of the squad stepped away from the doorway, instinctively looking for more heat. The logs cracked and crackled as the flames took hold.

"Will this work, Cap?" Wiggins said.

"It did in the hangar, lad," Banks said, trying to put some reassurance into it, although he wasn't sure he believed it himself. "It's all we've got, so get to it. Let's warm things up a bit around here."

*

The extent of the frost spread quickly, crawling along the walls as if being laid down by some invisible painter, creeping across the floor towards Banks' feet, tendrils reaching out, looking for prey.

He stepped further backward, trying to get even closer to the stove. Flames roared in the grate at his back but it seemed to give out little heat. In truth, he had never felt such cold, not even in the far north in the waters off Baffin Island. It was as if his blood thickened, freezing solid in his veins. A strange lethargy began to take him. He was looking at the doorway, but he saw stars, the infinite blackness, calling him to sweet oblivion. He took a step forward, towards the door rather than the fire, then another.

"Cap!" Hynd shouted and pulled Banks back towards the stove, putting his own body between the captain and the creeping ice. Banks' head cleared immediately, all compulsion gone as quickly as it had come.

"Thanks," he said to the sarge. He raised a hand, intending to pat Hynd on the arm, and saw to his dismay that his hands were almost as blue as those of the German Oberst outside. A thin layer of frost ran, all the way up to his wrists.

"Best warm your hands, Cap," Hynd said. "It's turned a bit on the nippy side."

Banks turned and faced the stove, feeling the heat tighten the skin across his cheeks. The frost on his hands quickly melted away, although it was going to take a bit longer for them to lose the blue tinge of cold. His blood began to move again, but he still felt sluggish.

The ice thickened on the inside surface of the door, freezing faster than the heat from the stove could melt it. Hughes' singing rose up from immediately outside the door.

And now these soldiers, these Scottish soldiers, who wandered far away and soldiered far away, see leaves are falling, and death is calling. And they will fade away in that far land.

"Fuck this shite, Cap," Wiggins said. "I'm a soldier, not a fucking ice cube tray. Open the door. Let's go down shooting."

"I'm not ready to give up yet. Stoke the flames, man. Keep stoking the flames. It's all that stands between us and a cold grave."

The fire had grown so as to fill the interior of the stove and there wasn't room for any more fuel. They had to stand back away from the waves of heat, but still the ice crept across the room towards them from the doorway and the squad huddled closer together in the space between the stove and the table.

"It's getting right cozy in here, Cap," Hynd said.

"Funny, that's what your wife said too," Wiggins replied.

The old familiar banter bought a round of laughter and raised their spirits. But the good humor didn't last for long. One by one, the men fell silent, each lost in his thoughts. The thudding on the door stopped, and now the only sound was to be heard was the crackle of the logs as the fire ate through fuel as fast as they could throw it on the flames.

But it seemed to be working. The spread of the ice slowed and finally it stopped six inches from their feet. It did not retreat, but Banks began to believe that they might yet survive this.

"Is it over, Cap?" Parker asked. Despite the heat, Banks saw that the private's lips were gray, almost blue, and that a layer of frost coated his thick eyebrows.

"Maybe aye, maybe no," Banks replied, hoping for one thing, fearing the other.

And then it came, the exact thing Banks had been dreading.

*

It started quietly again, the same far-off chanting, the monkish choir in the wind. Banks didn't know what was worse, a dead man singing, or this insistent, far too seductive plainsong.

"Earplugs," he said, loud enough for everyone to hear. "Plugs in now."

They all complied. For several minutes, the chanting seemed to recede and fade, but it was still getting louder, and eventually, the plugs weren't enough to mute the sound, and Banks felt the pull of the dance, the twitch in his muscles as they remembered the dark and the void.

"Dhumna Ort!" he muttered, hoping for the same protection as previously, but the chanting kept getting louder. The pounding came at the door again, keeping time with the beat, a rhythm that tuned into his breathing, his heartbeat, even the crackle of flame on the damp wood in the stove, everything dancing in time. He felt the tug and call of the infinite, knew that the stars and dark spaces were waiting a heartbeat away, and all he had to do was let it take him and all would be well. But it wasn't the stars he was seeing in his mind now – it was Patel, dark eyes pleading just before the German broke his neck.

"Dhumna Ort!" he shouted, and this time he got something, a certain distance from the relentless beat, a dimming of the chanting. He shouted the phrase again, and the distance between him and the darkness increased farther. Hynd had also got the message and he and Banks started into a chant of their own in an attempt to beat back that of the distant choir, the two words repeated over and over.

"Dhumna Ort!"

The ice that had been stopped six inches from their feet retreated, only by the width of a finger, but definitely noticeable.

"Come on, you buggers," Hynd shouted to the other three men, "join in. Or would you rather wait until your bollocks freeze off?"

It took several seconds before they all got it, but once the five of them chanted the words in unison, the ice retreated even faster. Their shouting, discordant as it was, muffled the monkish chanting, their stamping and clapping nullified the pounding at the door and sent the frost melting away from them across the floor leaving only damp floor behind it.

Banks almost yelled in triumph but could afford to break the rhythm of their chant. Besides, the closer the frost got to the doorway, the slower it retreated, until finally the retreat stopped where the foot of the door met the floor. Although the crawl of tendrils of frost on the walls had also disappeared, the ice on the surface of the door itself remained as thick as ever. They had reached an impasse, but had bought themselves time, and a larger area clear of the biting cold. But Banks knew that if they stopped chanting and stamping, or if the stove were allowed to burn any less fiercely then the ice – and the call of the stars – would be back in full measure. He kept shouting, kept clapping, and kept stamping.

"Dhumna Ort! Dhumna Ort!"

*

The night wore on. Banks' palms ached from the clapping, his ankles throbbed from the stamping, and his throat threatened to dry and close from the strain of the repetition of the Gaelic. He saw the same effort show on the faces of the others. But they all knew they could not afford to stop. That point was proved all too noticeably when McCally had to take a break in order to stoke the stove, which was in danger of not burning hard enough to keep the frost at bay. In the few seconds that the corporal's voice and clapping was not raised with the others, the frost crept in from the door, six inches closer across the hut floor, and Banks felt the bite of cold at his nose and cheeks.

He couldn't afford to stop his own shouting, but he saw the look that McCally gave him after throwing three more short-cut logs in the stove. The area under the stove itself was now almost empty.

We're running out of fuel.

There was no point in worrying about it. All they were able to do was keep up the shouting, clapping, and stamping and hope it was enough to keep the encroaching cold at bay. And if it wasn't, well, there was always Wiggins' option of opening the door and going at it all guns blazing. That was going to be Banks' last resort, but he was coming to think it might also be his last available option.

It wasn't long before McCally reached under the stove for more fuel and came up empty-handed. Banks didn't stop stamping or shouting, but stopped clapping long enough to motion at the table and chairs. Thankfully, the corporal got the message, and quickly kicked and stomped the chairs and table into timber small enough to be fed into the stove. But the new fuel wasn't as dense as the old logs, and burned faster. It was only ten minutes later that yet more fuel was needed. The frost grew another six inches across the floor as McCally and Parker tore planks and facing from the twin bunk beds and fed it into the flames.

*

Beds, bedclothes, shoring planks and all went to feed the ravenous stove, and all were too little to hold back the frost from creeping ever closer to their toes. The five men took turns, circling while stamping so that one of them was always closer to the stove and got a modicum of heat, for a time. But the spells between their turn at the warmth got colder, bitterly so, and despite their best efforts, they were all tiring now, their clapping and stomping and shouting not loud enough to drown the chanting.

As if sensing their weakened state, the thumping at the door started up again, and the frost crept faster across the floor, and also upward and outward, spreading along the walls in a spider-web crawl across the interior timbers.

Finally, McCally fed the last of their available fuel into the stove. Short of burning their own clothing and gear, there was no more they could do – all they had was the shouting, clapping, stamping, and what diminishing heat they could draw from the stove.

They kept circling.

*

Banks felt the cold with each breath when he wasn't the man nearest the stove, felt ice crackle at his lips. His feet were like lumps of cold stone and he couldn't feel his fingers when he clapped his hands. The monkish chanting was louder still and the tug of the darkness and the stars called hard now. Their shouting and clapping fell into the rhythm of a parade ground drill, and Banks put everything he had into it, one last effort. The others heard, and replied with a renewed burst of energy from all of them, but all they managed was to stop the ice coming any closer for a matter of minutes, and all too soon it had started to creep again.

All Banks knew was the stamping and circling, the clapping and the shouting.

"Dhumna Ort!" he uttered, barely able to manage much above a coarse rasp.

It wasn't enough. Slowly, remorselessly the cold crept in, reaching their toes, their heels and their ankles. They kept circling for a time, or at least it felt like they did, but gray crept into Banks' sight with the cold, gray that became black, a deep well that was filled with stars. He tried to remember what it was he should be doing, words he should be saying, but another rhythm had him now, a cold throbbing in the dark. He tasted salt water at his lips, saw the void spread out like a blanket in front of him.

He fell into it, lost in the dance.

- 13 -

Banks came out of it slowly, not where he might have expected to inside the saucer, but standing, still out in the open, in front of the locked door of the disguised hut, the metal door that led into the base. Thin watery light washed the sky, and as purple gave way to azure, so too the distant chanting faded, and so too did the compulsion to dance in the darkness.

The coming of day had saved them. Part of Banks, a large part if he was truthful to himself, was saddened to feel the dance leave him.

The five men were all groggy and looked at each other in bemusement. Banks felt the cold bite hard at his feet and ankles. It might be morning, but it was a bitter one. A snell wind cut through his clothing and blew ice and snow around the doorway. Wiggins and Parker had gloved hands on the wheel of the lock mechanism, as if they'd been in the process of opening the door just before waking. They had to prise their hands from the metal where the material of their gloves had frozen to the wheel.

"What the fuck, Cap," Wiggins said. "How the bloody hell did we get out here? It happened again, didn't it?"

"Aye," Banks replied. "But we fought it off. So don't go worrying about it. Back to the hut. We've got some thinking to do, but we need to get out of this weather; it looks like a storm coming in."

They turned away from the door and with Hynd and Banks in the lead made their way quickly back down the slope. Banks turned the corner to the doorway of the hut, and stopped so quickly that Parker walked into his back and nearly tumbled them both to the ground.

The hut door was wide open, but there was no space for the

squad inside; that was taken up by the dead, both the Germans, half a dozen of them…and three new recruits to their ranks in Wilkes, Patel, and Hughes. Wilkes showed no sign of the bloody wounds he'd taken in getting slammed into the hut wall. Like the other two, he now wore an immaculately clean uniform, as pristine as that worn by the German officer. The only difference now was that each of them sported the familiar Swastika armband on their left upper arm. The three dead men stood just behind the tall German oberst, and all four of them raised their arm in unison, and pointed. Banks didn't have to check the direction; he knew exactly where they wanted him to go.

"We can take them here and now, Cap," Hynd said at his shoulder. "Just give the word."

"No. We can't," Banks said. "That bastard has already proved that to us. What do they say – insanity is keeping doing the same thing and expecting different results? I'm done with that. And I'm not about to fire on my own men, dead or not. It's time for a new tack. And we might as well be warm while we think on it. Back to the hangar base, lads. And down to the living quarters."

Wiggins was the one to speak, but Banks knew most of them were thinking it.

"Bugger that for a game of soldiers, Cap. I'm pished off playing the hokey-cokey with these wee shitebags."

Banks pointed into the hut.

"I've lost three of you already. I'll be fucked if I'm losing anymore. Now get back to the hatch doorway. And in case you've forgotten your place, that's a fucking order, Private."

When Hynd called for them to move out, they all moved out. Banks was last to turn away. He had a final look at the three men – his men, his failure showing all too clear in the milk-white eyes. The sight of the Swastika band on their arms sickened him, as he knew it would have sickened them; now, it was just another taunt, another all too clear sign of how he had let them down. Their gaze bored into the back of his head as he walked away to join the remains of his squad.

*

At least he'd been right about one thing; it was considerably warmer inside the base, noticeably so even as they stepped inside the heavy metal door and closed it behind them. Wiggins moved to lock it internally, but Banks stopped him.

"Leave it, lad. Yon frozen buggers don't seem to be any respecters of locks, and our relief might need to come in fast, so let's not make it hard for them, eh?"

Wiggins looked like he wanted to say something, but Banks' rebuke several minutes earlier appeared to make him more circumspect this time, which suited Banks just fine. He didn't have time to be dealing with insubordination; he was too busy dealing with his own doubts.

They all moved down to the first landing. Banks unzipped his outer jacket and winced as his hands tingled with returning heat. He turned to Hynd.

"We're only going as far in as we need to go in order to get some heat and some rest. I don't want anyone going near that fucking saucer. We'll make for the living quarters then pick a nice wee warm room, and we stay there until the relief arrives. We've got some rations, some reading material, heat, and light. Everything a growing lad needs."

"Except the sarge's wife," Wiggins replied, but this time the humor fell flat. The squad had just seen their dead friends stand with the German officer, and it had affected them all. Banks pushed the image away as soon as he thought it. He realized he was locking an awful lot of stuff away in there, stuff that he knew would be back to bite him on the arse on long dark nights once they got home.

Aye, well, it can get in line with all the other crap.

*

He led the squad away, heading down into the bowels of the

base.

"In out, in out, shake it all about," Wiggins muttered, but nobody felt like singing along.

It felt warmer still in the main living chamber at the foot of the stairwell. The overhead lights glowed, not white as might be expected, but the same warm golden glow they'd encountered in the hangar around the saucer. Banks glanced at the double doorway that led to the hangar, and felt the pull and tug, the urge to join the dance.

"Dhumna Ort!" he muttered. He remembered how putting in his earplugs had muted the effect, and motioned to the others to follow his lead in pushing the plugs in deep.

"We're going to be shouting at each other with these things in, so keep chat to a minimum," he said. "Hand signals only, and speaking only if you really need to. Got it?"

Hynd pushed his plugs in and gave Banks the thumbs up. The other three followed suit. Banks was relieved to note that the urge to run through the double door and head for the hangar had now gone. He motioned to the team to get on the move.

They did a quick survey of the rooms, relieved to find they were all empty of cold corpses, and chose one with four bunks and a table and chairs. Banks got them inside, closed the door behind them, and motioned that the team should each take a bunk.

He sat down, suddenly dog-tired, at the table. The weight of the events of the day before, and the night they'd spent in the hut felt like a heavy stone pressing down on his shoulders. He put his head in his hands and was asleep before he could give any thought to setting a guard.

*

He dreamed, of starry vistas and swirling shadows, of nebulous gas clouds the size of galaxies, of the nurseries and graveyards of the stars themselves, and of dancing, lost and joyous in the rhythm of the black.

This time, he came out of it standing at the door of the room, his hand on the door handle – it had been the feel of cold metal in his palm that had brought him just far enough out of dream sleep to realize what was happening. Somewhere, far distant, a choir chanted in the wind, but now that he was awake, he found he could fight against it.

"Dhumna Ort!" he whispered, and all compulsion fell away from him, dispelled as quickly as the vanishing of the far-off chanting.

He looked around. The other four men were all asleep, Wiggins snoring loudly, Parker muttering and moaning, McCally lying half-in, half out of a cot as if he'd tried to get out of it then lost all energy, and Hynd, face down, breathing heavily. They all seemed to be genuinely asleep, but Banks couldn't help wondering if they too were somewhere off in the black, lost to the dance.

He let them sleep. He rummaged in his backpack and took out the old leather journal, needing something to focus on to stop sleep, and the dance, from leading him astray. He'd already read all of the account of the nature of the thing in the submarine, but perhaps there was something else in the writings that could help him understand – and maybe even overcome – what they were dealing with here. One word, 'demon' caught his attention as he scanned the pages, and he backed up a few pages, and started reading at that point.

*

As I descended the steps, I got a clue as to what Churchill had meant. There had been a fire in the area under the bar at some point in the past, not recently, but one that had been bad enough to leave a thick layer of ash and soot covering everything. Light came in through a small window high up that was itself smeared with a greasy film of thin soot. The window overlooked the river, and despite the soot was letting in enough light for me to see that I wasn't in a beer cellar after all.

The fire that had left the soot and ash behind had also left remnants of furniture: three long sofas, all halfway burned through, and a squat square table that had been overturned and leaned against the wall.

A roughly circular piece of the floorboards, a yard or so at the widest point had been cleared of ash, and I got my first inkling of why Churchill had asked for my help. I could not see all of it, but there was definitely a magic circle and an interior pentagram drawn there.

But this wasn't one of my protections, far from it. I had seen the like of this before, in books in my library, old books, that dealt with calling up all manner of things to do your bidding. This was a summoning circle, and from the quick look I'd had at it, I had a sinking feeling it wasn't mere necromancy that had been attempted in this room.

Whoever had been at work here was after something rather more sensational. It was clear to me now that they had been involved in a medieval ritual of some infamy; this room had seen an attempt at summoning, and controlling, a demon.

Of course, I know there are no such things as demons, there are merely mischief making manifestations from the Outer Darkness. But people who dabble in the esoteric disciplines without any training are wont to see what they expect, especially those of a religious bent to start with. I had no doubt that this small room here under the bar had seen some excitable people get excited, perhaps even over excited while under the influence of drugs and liquor and the promise of power from the great beyond.

While I'd been examining the circle and arriving at some conclusions as to its nature, Churchill had been watching me.

"First impressions, old boy?" he asked.

"Stuff and nonsense," I replied. "People with more money and liquor than sense looking for an easy thrill, and receiving precisely what they were looking for. It's all parlor games and cheap tricks to rook the gullible. You're a man of the world, Churchill; you know that for yourself."

Churchill nodded.

"I have usually been of the same mind," he replied, "despite having come across several things on my travels over the years that have as yet defied explanation. And, like you, I would put this down to too much liquor, money, and high spirits. But there is more to it than that; otherwise, I would not have bothered you with it in the first place."

"More?" I said, looking around at the burned remains of the room and the marks on the floor. "What more could there possibly be?"

"Just wait," Churchill replied. He hadn't put out his cigar, and he chewed on it as he spoke. I sensed tension in him, a rare thing to see in a man who was normally so self-assured, and I wondered what might be the cause. Then a cloud went over the sun outside the only window, and I saw exactly what had brought on his uncharacteristic nervousness.

A dark, shadowy figure stood inside the circle on the floor, insubstantial, like something produced by smoke and mirrors. It wasn't quite as tall as a man, more child-like in stature and stance, and one that appeared to be bent and twisted, as if all the bones in its body had been broken, then imperfectly set.

It took several seconds before my eyes adjusted to the growing gloom, and it was only then that I got my first clear look, and saw that it was not human, not even remotely. It was reddish in color, appearing almost as burned as the room in which we stood, and it maintained its balance in the circle with the aid of a pair of large, leathery, wings that stretched out from its shoulders and fanned the stale air around. It stared at me from dark, almost black, eyes and I felt an involuntary shiver run through me.

For all intents and purposes, I was looking into the eyes of a demon.

It did not speak, for which I was grateful, but it stared at me most balefully. It opened and closed small fists, gripping with long, slender fingers, as if it wished it had them affixed around my neck. A tongue flicked from the thin black lips; I did not have *time to check if it was forked at the end, for at that moment the cloud moved on outside, the sun reappeared, and the figure in the circle became thin and unsubstantial once again, before fading away completely.*

"I do not believe in demons," I said, mostly to reassure myself that I had not, in fact, witnessed what I had seen.

Churchill laughed.

"I don't think he cares, old man."

*

Demons again, and Churchill again, but nothing that could help Banks in his quest for clarity here.

"I don't believe in demons," he muttered, repeating the words he'd just read, but he couldn't make himself believe it after all that he'd seen since their arrival at the base. He started to close the journal, but knew that would only leave him alone with his thoughts, and vulnerable to the call from the darkness. Reading had been helping to keep it at bay, so he skipped forward a few pages until he encountered the word again, and read on from there.

*

It did not take long for the demon, if that was indeed what it was, to show itself again. It started to come into view almost as soon as I switched off the lamp and the wash of colors from my valves only emboldened it and brought it ever more into solid reality.

I sat on the step and watched it closely, trying to ascertain if it had any sense of purpose or intent, but it was more in the nature of a moving image, albeit a solid one, rather than anything with any degree of intelligence of its own.

The circle in which it stood was another matter entirely. Its lines and daubs, primitive though they might be, exerted a definite opposing force against my valves, and it sent out a darkness that tried to dim the pentacle's brightness and infected the colors with a pinkish-red hue that was almost fiery.

I picked up my small control box and started to modulate the valves, rotating through various pulses and color combinations, searching for one that might defend, and even repel, the red darkness that tried to ooze from the original circle. But in doing so, I almost brought about my own downfall. I discovered that if I used too little blue, or too much red, the strength of the inner circle swelled ever stronger.

It pressed hard against the valves, causing all of them to whine and complain even as I tried to switch to a different modulation. It was as I was attempting to turn up the yellow that I saw the thing that worried me.

The oozing red color thickened inside the original circle, flaring like a raging fire. The demon, no longer quite so static as before, danced in the flame, no longer grinning but screaming soundlessly as if burning in great agony. I felt a blast of heat reach me, even protected as I was by the circles of my electric pentacle. There was also a warm glow on my face, like sun on a hot summer's day, but it was as nothing compared to what appeared to be hungry fires lapping all around the now thrashing red figure that was imprisoned right in the center of all the commotion.

As I increased the power to the yellow valve, more demonic figures in the center circle showed solid form. Indeed, it was soon packed tight with them, a throng, a horde, of cavorting, red figures packed together so tightly that they stood shoulder to shoulder, completely filling the space inside the circle, all screaming as they burned in hellish flame. And even as I had the thought, I knew what I was seeing; I was indeed looking beyond a veil to part of the great beyond I had not previously encountered.

I believe I was being given a vision of Hell itself.

Not that I believed in a literal Hell of course, but I knew that old tales, religion, and mythology often had their origins in glimpses of compartments or realms of Outer Darkness that the human mind had to try to rationalize to understand them. Perhaps Hell as understood by the wider world was always merely a construct built to make sense of a glimpse of somewhere else, a door through to this burning, red horror I was currently watching.

Wherever it was, the older, inner circle was still exuding heat and the room was heating up by the second. I was starting to wonder whether the fire that had consumed the cellar ten years before had been intentional at all. I did not have time to dwell on it, for if it got any hotter, I was going to have to beat a hasty retreat to avoid ending up in the northern sanitarium alongside the last man to see the same sight.

I pushed the yellow valve to as high a brightness as I dared, and that did seem to bring a momentary coolness wafting through the cellar, but any respite was short-lived, and within seconds the red flames lashed harder still against the pentacle. I quickly went through several more permutations of color and modulation as the heat grew almost unbearable and almost cried out in relief when, just as I thought I would have to flee, I set a wave of rapid alternating pulses of blue and yellow washing through the room.

The fires inside the circle dimmed and faded as if doused by water. The demons screamed soundlessly, threw their limbs around in a jerky, almost comical, dance, then they too dimmed and went quiet, leaving only the original, winged beast standing in the center. It looked at me and it appeared to be smiling as it too finally faded and dissipated before disappearing entirely, leaving me alone in a room awash with blue and yellow and a cool, almost chill breeze that came through the wall of the river beyond.

I sat still, watching, for the length of time it took to smoke two cheroots, leaving the pentacle running. The only sound was the hum from my battery and the thin whine that came from the valves as they dimmed and faded. The washes of color splashed across wall, ceiling, and floor, but that was the only movement to be seen. There was no reappearance of any demon, dancing *or otherwise, in the inner circle.*

After my smokes, I lit my oil lamp again and switched off the pentacle, ready to switch it back on at the first sign of any redness or flame. The cellar remained quiet and cool. And I realized something else. It felt empty, and somehow I knew for a fact that I was the only presence here.

*

Banks sat up straight in the chair, suddenly hit by inspiration that had eluded him until now. The golden circles and markings on the floor weren't the cause of the problems on the base; his reading had just made that clear.

The circles are attempts to contain the demon, possibly even an attempt to control it. The saucer is sitting in a prison the Germans made for it.

It had held all these long years from the war until now. But somehow, the bonds that held the demon had been slipped, if only a fraction. And now whatever lived in that prison was trying its best to escape.

*

He let the men sleep while he sat at the table, pondering his epiphany. He couldn't make heads or tails of the talk in the journal of color washes and valves, at least none that would help him. From what he could gather, the man, Carnacki, had a piece of equipment that he used in his work that utilized the color theory mentioned, but as they'd found no sign of any such equipment on the base, Banks didn't think the Germans had used the same methods.

He looked for the other bag of papers before remembering that it must still be back in the hut; he hadn't seen it recently, hadn't given it any thought, and now that he needed it, it was in the one place he couldn't, wouldn't go to fetch. He remembered that it had been occult symbols he hadn't understood, blueprints for building the saucer, and those, impossible, shots of the saucer in orbit. It all added up to something that he thought he should understand, but which remained too far away from how he'd always understood the world worked.

But merely the fact that the demon could be controlled, even expelled, gave Banks hope, and that was something that had been in short supply this past twenty-four hours.

*

He sat there, wide-awake now, idly reading passages from Carnacki's journal. The man had obviously had dealings with Churchill, and knew something about all this demonic mumbo-jumbo, but it was like reading a fairytale for all the sense it made to Banks. He could see nothing that would be really useful in bringing their situation to an end.

He was still of a mind to sit this one out, wait for the relief and tell them his theory, but any thought of an easy time of it was thwarted after a few hours of respite. It started, as before, with a high chanting, monks singing in the wind.

Banks quickly roused the men.

"Get the plugs full in, lads," he said, almost shouting so that they'd hear him. "And remember the Gaelic. It's the only thing that saved us before. Get ready to move."

"We're not going back outside again, surely, Cap," Wiggins replied. "We've only just got fucking warm."

It was only on hearing the question that Banks realized he'd come to a decision while sitting in the quiet room.

"No. We're not heading out," he said. "We're heading in. It's time to face this thing. This ends now, one way or the other."

- 14 -

He led the men out into the main chamber. As soon as he opened the room door, the sound of the chanting got noticeably louder, even through the earplugs.

"Dhumna Ort!" he muttered, which helped, but didn't deaden the sound entirely anymore. He motioned the men forward, and was pleased to see that they had all unslung their weapons, and had fallen into formation behind him. Hynd brought up the rear as Banks led the other three quickly across the large empty space to the double doorway that led to the hangar corridor.

He realized he had no clear plan, but it felt good to be on the move again, and with a definite goal in mind. The first step was to get to the saucer room. He was hoping something else would come to him by the time they got there.

*

The heat in the corridor beyond the double doors was almost stifling, but Banks wasn't of a mind to divest himself of his outerwear – the experience in the hut had impressed on him just how quickly the temperature might change. It was getting uncomfortably sweaty inside his gear, but it was a small price to pay if it stopped him turning like the dead men he'd seen with the Oberst.

But they wouldn't be able to put up with such heat for long, for it was going to sap their strength just as fast as any prolonged exposure to the cold. He headed up the corridor at double time. The chanting got louder, it got hotter, and Banks wasn't quite sure if he was running into action, or running to answer the call of the dark void of eternity.

As long as we get to the bloody hangar room, the why of it doesn't really matter.

He kept telling himself that, but wasn't sure he believed it.

*

The hangar room glowed as golden yellow, and as warm, as any midday summer sun, and the saucer hummed and vibrated, as if excited at their approach. One thing changed as soon as they entered the hangar – the chanting stopped again, and all compulsion left Banks.

We're where it wants us to be. Again.

Banks pulled out his earplugs, and the squad followed suit when they saw.

"Cally," Banks said. "Can we cut the power?"

"Cut it? I don't even know where it's coming from – or going to," the corporal said.

Banks nodded toward the saucer.

"We can assume it's coming from there," he said, then walked over to the tall metal containers banked beside the gauges and meters, "and it's going here, then out to the rest of the base."

"I get that much," McCally said, "but what's powering yon fucker?"

Banks looked back at the saucer.

"I think we are. I think we have been since we got here."

"So what's the plan, Cap?" Hynd asked.

"There's two bits of it," Banks said. "The first is easy – we cool things down around here; cut off the power leaving the saucer, stop it heating this room and the rest of the base. Let's see if we can stir things up, take the initiative."

McCally looked at the tall metal containers again.

"Breaking stuff and blowing shit up? Aye, I can do that."

He took Parker and Wiggins with him and went over to the tall metal containers. It took all three of them, but once they put their combined weight into it, they got the racks of containers on the move. One last effort, a heave from all of them, and the whole row toppled forward and crashed to the floor with an impact that shook the whole hangar and made the saucer wobble where it hovered.

Another effect was also immediate. The lights went out in the corridor beyond the double doorway, and a cold breeze blew up from the rest of the base. The yellow glow from the circles on the floor faded to their previous gold, the radiated heat from them no longer so oppressive as before.

"Still too warm by half," Banks said. He caught sight of shadows moving across the floor and looked up. Snow swirled in spiraling vortices outside the glass of the dome, and now that the chanting had stopped, and his plugs were out, he heard the whistle and roar of the wind.

"There's a storm out there, lads," he said. "Let's get some of it in here."

He raised his weapon, pointing at the dome. As the rest of the squad followed his lead, they heard another sound, not from outside, but from back down in the base itself, a loud metallic clanging.

"We're about to have company again, lads," Banks said. "Let's give them a welcome."

He aimed upward at the glass between the iron supports of the dome and sent three quick shots into it. The rest of the squad fired only a second behind him. The glass shattered immediately, shards falling around them like icicles.

The storm took full advantage, roaring into the hangar like a caged beast, suddenly freed.

- 15 -

The glow from the circles diminished still further, and the saucer sank slowly downward, still hovering, but now merely inches off the ground again.

"It's working, Cap," Parker shouted.

"Aye, maybe. But is it working enough?"

They had to zip up their jackets and pull their hoods over their heads – the wind bit hard, with snow flurries spattering in their faces, rasping at their skin like sandpaper.

"Hynd, you take Cally and Parker and watch that doorway. If those fucking popsicles show up, keep them out in the corridor as long as you can. Only fall back inside the circles as a last resort. Clear?"

"Aye, aye, cap," Hynd replied, and gave a mock salute.

"What about me, Cap?" Wiggins said.

"You're with me, lad."

"Are we going somewhere?"

"You might say that, aye," Banks replied. "Let's see if your flying is any better than your driving."

"What the fuck, Cap?"

Banks smiled.

"That's the second part of the plan. We call its bluff. We're going in. It wants us to fly the fucker, let's fly the fucker."

He didn't wait to see if Wiggins would follow him. If the private showed hesitation, it might have weakened Banks' own resolve, and it was weak enough already. He stepped over toward the outer of the golden circles. The chanting came again, the monks shouting in the wind. This time, he did not put in the earplugs, but welcomed the song into him.

As he stepped into the circles, he heard Hynd call out from

behind him.

"We've got incoming."

Wiggins stepped up beside him. The door in the saucer cracked, creaked, and fell open to their touch.

They stepped up into the saucer at almost the same moment as the squad opened fire in the doorway.

- 16 -

Banks didn't hesitate. He went straight to the pentacles on the floor near the long window and stepped into the right hand one. Wiggins followed him and took the left pentacle.

The chanting rose in volume. Dark shadows swirled around the two men, thick as velvet drapes, dampening, almost drowning, the sound of shooting from out in the hangar.

"You weren't serious about flying this fucker, were you, Cap?" Wiggins asked. He sounded far away, almost as distant as the chanting that continued to grow louder, more insistent.

"Not if we can shut it off first," Banks said.

"How does this fucker work? There's nae fucking controls, Cap."

"We think hard at it – at least that's the general idea. I ken that's not your strong point, lad, but help me out here."

"Just tell me what to think," Wiggins said, and Banks laughed.

"Lad, you've been in service for too long. But that's the easy bit. We want this fucker quiet; dead and still on the floor like when we got here. So, sleepy thoughts, keep it quiet, and let's get this thing shut off."

*

Banks tried to concentrate on the same thing he'd told Wiggins, but quiet was a long way away. Despite the dampening effect inside the saucer, the sound of gunfire was still clear, and Banks could not erase the worry he felt for the three men he'd left outside.

It appeared Wiggins felt the same for, unbidden, the saucer

moved. It did not descend to the floor, but swung around, so that they looked out of the window at the scene in the doorway.

"Did you do that, Cap?" Wiggins said.

"I thought you did."

Then both fell quiet. The tall German officer stood in the doorway, and the three dead squad members stood at his shoulder. Hynd, Parker, and McCally backtracked, firing round after round into the iced dead but doing no sign of any damage. The oberst looked up at the saucer, straight at the window, directly at Banks. His eyes were no longer milky, but flaring fiery red, and his skin, once blue, had taken on a hint of burnt ochre. Dark shadows swirled behind him, almost obscuring the dead squad members, shadows that furled and unfurled, like great wings ready to take flight.

"What the fuck, Cap?" Wiggins muttered.

"Steady, lad. We're seeing what it expects us to see, that's all. We didn't start thinking about red-eyed demons until I read about it in that fucking journal. This fucker is in my head. I hope it likes the mess I've made in there over the years."

The squad continued to backtrack, still shooting while the iced dead came through the doorway, matching their pace to the retreating men. The tall oberst never took his gaze from the window, as if it knew Banks was watching. Banks had another epiphany.

It wants us all inside the circles. It can draw more power that way.

The chanting of the monks got louder. Banks felt the call of the dark, saw the shadows swirl darker, and stars appear in the blackness. The void opened out all around the pentacles where they stood.

Outside, the oberst took another step toward the retreating men. They were almost backed up against the outer circle.

"Bugger this for a lark. Up," Banks shouted to Wiggins. "Take us up."

"What? Are you daft, man?"

"That's a fucking order, Private," he shouted. "Fly this

fucker out of here, right now, before it takes us all."

Banks thought about the saucer, glowing brighter, and rising off the hangar floor. It appeared that Wiggins took his order to heart, for it felt like his own thoughts were amplified, boosted, and the view out of the window changed as the saucer rose, slowly at first, then definitely accelerating upward.

The tall oberst looked into Banks' eyes. The last thing Banks saw before the view of the hangar slipped out of sight completely was the German's lips raise in a smile, and a black, forked, tongue slither out between them.

- 17 -

The dance washed over Banks in a wave of blackness and void, starless and bible-black at first, then slowly taking form as they drifted with the beat. Part of him was aware that he still stood inside a pentacle, on the floor of a golden saucer, hovering now above the broken fragments of a shattered dome.

But that part was insignificant compared to the vastness of the void, and the call of the dance. Banks wanted to fall into it, to let it take him off and into the deep dark, where there was nothing but the dance, and peace, forever.

I want this.

And with it came realization.

This is what I want. It's what I have always wanted, in my heart. The fucker is still inside my head. And it wants something else.

He tasted salt water at his lips, and remembered how Carnacki had stood, alone in the dark, remembered where Churchill had found his 'demon.' He had a final epiphany.

"Wiggins," he shouted into the dark. "Go left. Ten feet then head for the door."

"Then what, Cap?" the private's voice came from everywhere and nowhere, a boom like the voice of God in the dark.

"Then jump. Jump if you want to live."

He felt the assisted boost of Wiggins' thought that, along with his own, moved the saucer slightly to one side, away from the shattered roof of the dome.

"Jump, Private, that's a fucking order," Banks shouted, and, judging to luck, left the pentacle at a straight run, heading for what he hoped was the doorway.

*

He met Wiggins just as his vision cleared. They almost wedged each other into the doorway. The second it took them to disentangle themselves was almost the end of them both; the saucer started to accelerate, heading toward the sea.

Banks didn't hesitate. He threw Wiggins out the open doorway, then jumped through after him.

The fall seemed to take forever.

- 18 -

He hit soft snow over hard ice, landing on his back, and was able to turn just in time to see the saucer hit the surface of the sea far out in the bay. It skipped like a flat stone, twice, before breaking apart with a screech of tearing metal that echoed around the cliffs.

At the last, as it sank a black shadow, wings unfurled, spread out across the surface, then slowly sank away. A fresh squall of wind and snow came in, passed over and when it cleared, there was nothing to see but the sea itself. The last thing to go was the far-off sound, monks chanting, not in the wind as Banks had thought, but from somewhere deep – deep, dark, and dancing in the abyssal swell, with the taste of salt water at their lips.

*

He was trying to pull Wiggins out of a snowdrift when the three remaining members of his squad came up the slope at a run. Wiggins' eyes were fluttering – he had taken a blow to the head and wasn't fully conscious, but there didn't appear to be any broken bones.

Hynd reached them first.

"I don't know what you did, Cap, but it fucking worked. There's nothing left but dirty freezing water down there."

Banks heard a new noise. He looked out over the sea again. The icebreaker was coming around the farthest point on the right side of the bay, and the distant whop of the heavy engines of a dinghy in the water echoed all around the cliffs.

"I sent the fucker where it wanted to go all along, ever since it was trapped on that Jerry sub all those years ago."

"And where was that, Cap?"

"Home. I sent it home."

*

They were all on the quay waiting by the time the dinghy came alongside. Wiggins, still semi-conscious, hung held upright between Hynd and McCally, and they moved quickly to get him into the dinghy as soon as it reached the dock. A bespectacled, bearded man that Banks took for the expert got out of the dinghy, took one look up at the shattered dome, and looked back at Banks in disgust.

"You call this sanitizing?"

"You're fucking welcome," Banks replied.

"That's what the sarge's wife says too," Wiggins replied.

THE END

CHECK OUT OTHER GREAT HORROR NOVELS

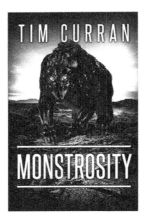

MONSTROSITY
by Tim Curran

The Food. It seeped from the ground, a living, gushing, teratogenic nightmare. It contaminated anything that ate it, causing nature to run wild with horrible mutations, creating massive monstrosities that roam the land destroying towns and cities, feeding on livestock and human beings and one another. Now Frank Bowman, an ordinary farmer with no military skills, must get his children to safety. And that will mean a trip through the contaminated zone of monsters, madmen, and The Food itself. Only a fool would attempt it. Or a man with a mission.

THE SQUIRMING
by Jack Hamlyn

You are their hosts.

You are their food.

The parasites came out of nowhere, squirming horrors that enslaved the human race. They turned the population into mindless pack animals, psychotic cannibalistic hordes whose only purpose was to feed them.

Now with the human race teetering at the edge of extinction, extermination teams are fighting back, killing off the parasites and their voracious hosts. Taking them out one by one in violent, bloody encounters.

The future of mankind is at stake.

And time is running out.

CHECK OUT OTHER GREAT
HORROR NOVELS

BLACK FRIDAY
by Michael Hodges

Jared the kleptomaniac, Chike the unemployed IT guy, Patricia the shopaholic, and Jeff the meth dealer are trapped inside a Chicago supermall on Black Friday. Bridgefield Mall empties during a fire alarm, and most of the shoppers drive off into a strange mist surrounding the mall parking lot. They never return. Chike and his group try calling friends and family, but their smart phones won't work, not even Twitter. As the mist creeps closer, the mall lights flicker and surge. Bulbs shatter and spray glass into the air. Unsettling noises are heard from within the mist, as the meth dealer becomes unhinged and hunts the group within the mall. Cornered by the mist, and hunted from within, Chike and the survivors must fight for their lives while solving the mystery of what happened to Bridgefield Mall. Sometimes, a good sale just isn't worth it.

GRIMWEAVE
by Tim Curran

In the deepest, darkest jungles of Indochina, an ancient evil is waiting in a forgotten, primeval valley. It is patient, monstrous, and bloodthirsty. Perfectly adapted to its hot, steaming environment, it strikes silent and stealthy, it chosen prey: human. Now Michael Spiers, a Marine sniper, the only survivor of a previous encounter with the beast, is going after it again. Against his better judgement, he is made part of a Marine Force Recon team that will hunt it down and destroy it.

The hunters are about to become the hunted.

CHECK OUT OTHER GREAT HORROR NOVELS

DEATH CRAWLERS
by Gerry Griffiths

Worldwide, there are thought to be 8,000 species of centipede, of which, only 3,000 have been scientifically recorded. The venom of Scolopendra gigantea—the largest of the arthropod genus found in the Amazon rainforest—is so potent that it is fatal to small animals and toxic to humans. But when a cargo plane departs the Amazon region and crashes inside a national park in the United States, much larger and deadlier creatures escape the wreckage to roam wild, reproducing at an astounding rate. Entomologist, Frank Travis solicits small town sheriff Wanda Rafferty's help and together they investigate the crash site. But as a rash of gruesome deaths befalls the townsfolk of Prospect, Frank and Wanda will soon discover how vicious and cunning these new breed of predators can be. Meanwhile, Jake and Nora Carver, and another backpacking couple, are venturing up into the mountainous terrain of the park. If only they knew their fun-filled weekend is about to become a living nightmare!

THE PULLER
by Michael Hodges

Matt Kearns has two choices: fight or hide. The creature in the orchard took the rest. Three days ago, he arrived at his favorite place in the world, a remote shack in Michigan's Upper Peninsula. The plan was to mourn his father's death and figure out his life. Now he's fighting for it. An invisible creature has him trapped. Every time Matt tries to flee, he's dragged backwards by an unseen force. Alone and with no hope of rescue, Matt must escape the Puller's reach. But how do you free yourself from something you cannot see?

Printed in Great Britain
by Amazon

64412200R00081